CARTOONISTS AGAINST THE HOLOCAUST

> **For information about ordering copies of *Cartoonists Against The Holocaust* for your school, organization or bookstore, or for a free downloadable PDF of the Teacher's Guide, please visit Clizia.com.**

ISBN: 978-0-692-47853-0

July 2015. First printing. *Cartoonists Against the Holocaust* is © 2015 Clizia, Inc. All Rights Reserved, including the digital remastering of the material not held by copyright owners.

To the best of the authors' and the publisher's knowledge all the cartoons and photographs used in this book are in the Public Domain and/or are permitted to be used under Fair Use. If we have not properly credited any legal holders we offer our sincere apologies and we very much welcome corrections to be gratefully made in future editions.

Any similarities to persons living or dead apart from historical figures are purely coincidental. With the exception of artwork used for review purposes, none of the contents of this publication may be reprinted without the permission of Clizia, Inc.

Clizia, Inc. is a Trade Mark of Clizia, Inc.

CARTOONISTS AGAINST THE HOLOCAUST

RAFAEL MEDOFF ■ CRAIG YOE

PRODUCED BY CLIZIA GUSSONI

ACKNOWLEDGMENTS

We are deeply grateful for the assistance we received from many friends, colleagues, and associates in the preparation of this book. Yael Fischer, Michael Herman, Eliyahu Korn, Ayelet Krieger, Shira Medoff, and Elliot Zolin assisted at various stages in the years-long search for cartoons. Irvin Ungar, president of the Arthur Szyk Society, helped identify and provide Szyk's cartoons. Several cartoons were located in periodicals generously donated to the David S. Wyman Institute for Holocaust Studies by the family of Herbert Romerstein. Dan Pattir, one of Israel's foremost authorities on cartoon history, lent his expertise and vast collection to help us pinpoint appropriate cartoons from the 1940s Hebrew-language press. Nicole C. Dittrich of Syracuse University Library's Special Collections Research Center and Tina Weiss of Hebrew Union College-Jewish Institute of Religion arranged access to important research collections.

Additional leads and assistance were provided by Lucy Shelton Caswell of The Ohio State University Billy Ireland Cartoon Library & Museum; Megan Garnett of the Newseum; George Hagenauer; Allan Holtz; Alan Kaplan; Martha H. Kennedy, Curator of Popular & Applied Graphic Art in the Prints and Photographs Division of the Library of Congress; Dr. Steven Luckert of the United States Holocaust Memorial Museum; Christine Neulieb of *Commonweal;* Jane Newton, of the Centre for the Study of Cartoons and Caricature at the University of Kent; and Abby Wisse.

Many of the cartoonists represented in this book were not well known at the time, and are even less so today, making basic biographical information hard to come by. Professor Rob Stolzer, chairman of the Department of Art & Design at the University of Wisconsin, helped in this effort, as did Hila Zahavi of the Israeli Museum of Caricature and Comics. Dr. Elvira Groezinger and Ralf Schulte were very helpful in our search for the elusive Eric Godal.

The process through which cartoons by Carl Rose were included in this book is a story all its own. The sleuthing skills of Susan Karlin, applied to an original cartoon (that was generously donated to the Wyman Institute by Steve Donnelly of Cool Lines Artwork), led us to numerous important Rose cartoons. Darryl Dick, working with Laurel Wolfson of Hebrew Union College-Jewish Institute of Religion, then arranged for crucial scans to be made available.

The idea for this book grew out of a traveling exhibit of the same name that the Wyman Institute created with the generous assistance of the late comic book legend Joe Kubert; his son, comics artist Adam Kubert; J. David Spurlock of Vanguard Productions; and Rob Shechter. The Westchester Holocaust and Human Rights Education Center, first under executive director Donna Cohen and educational director Dr. Marlene Yahalom, and then led by executive director Millie Jasper and educational codirectors Julie Scallero and Steven Goldberg, sponsored the exhibit at numerous schools in Westchester County, NY. Lawrence Klein and Sandy Schechter (assisted by Ken Wong) of the Museum of Comic and Cartoon Art arranged for the exhibit to appear at their museum as well.

Many thanks to our fact-checkers and proofreaders: Karen Green, Mark Lerer, Peter Sanderson, and Steven Thompson.

But most of all, our deepest gratitude to Clizia Gussoni whose expertise and dedication to this book made it a reality.

CONTENTS

Introduction 7

1. Hitler Comes To Power 13
2. Symbols of Hate 23
3. Burning Books, Burning People 29
4. Minister of Hate: Joseph Goebbels 35
5. Teaching Children to Hate 41
6. The Nazification of the Universities 45
7. Hitler on Trial 49
8. Racism as a Way of Life 51
9. The Cold Pogrom 57
10. The Nuremberg Laws 61
11. Doing Business with Hitler 65
12. Aryanization 69
13. The League of Nations 73
14. The Nazi Olympics 75
15. Nazism Spreads 81
16. Hitler's Move into Austria 85
17. Paper Walls 93
18. A Refugee Conference that Abandoned the Refugees 97
19. Appeasing Hitler 99
20. Kristallnacht: Shattered Glass—and Shattered Lives 105
21. The World's Response to Kristallnacht 113
22. Kristallnacht and Christianity 119
23. No Room for Children 125
24. Escape to Freedom 127
25. The White Paper 131

26. Voyage of the Doomed	133
27. World War II Begins	139
28. The Holocaust Begins	143
29. The "Liberation" that Wasn't	147
30. Dr. Seuss and the Holocaust	151
31. Genocide Confirmed	153
32. The Gas Chambers	155
33. Trains of Death	159
34. Bermuda: the Mock Refugee Conference	163
35. A Dramatic Rescue from Denmark	165
36. Fighting Back	167
37. FDR and the Holocaust	171
38. The Holocaust Rages On	177
39. Hunting Jews	183
40. The Holocaust Reaches Hungary	185
41. "Free Ports" for Cans of Beans—and for People	189
42. What Kind of Peace?	193
43. Judgement Day	195
About the Cartoonists	201
Index to Cartoonists	205
Source Notes	207
Index	209
About the Authors	212

INTRODUCTION

Thomas Nast, the father of American political cartooning, circa 1860s.

It has been said that 90% of what we learn comes through the "eye gate," not, as one might suppose, the "ear gate." Pictures have the power to lodge themselves in our brains, stimulate our thinking and feelings, and finally motivate our actions. Cartoonists understand that the strength of their work comes through combining formidable ideas, carefully planned compositions, and skillful renderings. All these elements make their cartoons engaging to the viewers.

When people think of a cartoonist, they often imagine someone who draws superhero comic books, a cartoon animator, or an artist who draws comic strips for newspapers or the Internet. But if the word "political" is placed before the word "cartoonist," an entirely different picture comes to mind. A political or editorial cartoonist pokes, prods, and provokes politicians and rallies the public to do the same. This kind of artist makes pen-and-ink sermons to get across a viewpoint, change people's perceptions, and, hopefully, improve society.

The political cartooning profession has enjoyed a long and colorful history. The very first political cartoonists probably scrawled on cave walls to make fun of whichever Neanderthal was in charge of keeping the newly-invented wheels of progress from turning. Post-cave-dwelling cartoonists have been credited with toppling kings and electing presidents. Those in power have reacted sometimes with amusement and sometimes by railing against these artists, banning their work, suing them, torturing them, or putting them in prison or concentration camps. Some contemporary political cartoonists even have had their lives threatened and been forced to go into hiding.

In January 2015, the saga of cartoonists and their opponents took a hideous new turn when Islamist terrorists massacred six editors and artists in the offices of the French satirical newspaper *Charlie Hebdo*. The killers said they were taking revenge for *Charlie Hebdo's* publication of cartoons that were offensive to Islam. With one swift, terrible burst of machine-gun fire, the world was reminded of the power of cartoons and the rage they can inspire—and the need for vigilance to ensure the freedoms we cherish.

America's first great cartoonist was Thomas Nast. In the late 1800s, Nast's drawings pointedly made fun of "Boss" Tweed, a corrupt New York City politician. Tweed sent his henchmen to lean on Nast, telling them, "Stop them damned pictures. I don't care so much what the papers say about me. My constituents don't know how to read, but they can't help seeing them damned pictures!" Eventually, Tweed was brought down by Nast's political cartooning and fled to Spain—only to be arrested by border guards who recognized him from Nast's cartoons!

Walt Kelly, the political satirist and creator of the famous comic strip *Pogo*, once compared a political cartoonist's role in society to that of a watchdog: "It is the duty of a watchdog to growl warnings, to bark, to surmise that every strange footfall is that of a cat, to worry about birds, and to suspect unknown insects."

Edmund Duffy's "Maryland, My Maryland."

America needed those watchdogs more than ever during the years of the Holocaust, when the Nazis and their collaborators murdered six million European Jews.

Too many Americans preferred to look away from what the Nazis were doing. It wasn't America's problem, they said. We had enough of our own worries. Maybe they weren't being treated as badly as some people claimed.

Some of those attitudes were driven by prejudice, some by ignorance, and some by selfishness. But whatever the motives, there was an urgent need to stir the public, to make people sit up and pay attention—and to do something. Millions of innocent lives were at stake. Someone had to sound the alarm. A number of cartoonists rose to the occasion, "barking" furiously in a desperate attempt to alert the public and their government to the plight of the Jews in Europe.

It's worth noting that these cartoonists were working in a professional environment that—to put it charitably—did not distinguish itself in its response to the Nazi genocide. Most major daily newspapers reported very little about the Holocaust or, at best, relegated that news to the back pages.

The cartoonists represented in these pages were the exceptions. While many editors, reporters, and, yes, editorial cartoonists were largely indifferent to the plight of the Jews, these courageous individuals chose to use their art in the service of humanity.

There was Edmund Duffy, the longtime editorial cartoonist for the *Baltimore Sun*, of whom the newspaper's editor, H.L. Mencken, once said: "Give me a good cartoonist and I can throw out half the editorial staff." Duffy, a three-time Pulitzer Prize winner, often stirred controversy with his ardent advocacy of civil rights. A 1931 cartoon by Duffy graphically depicting the recent lynching of an African-American man, sarcastically titled "Maryland, My Maryland" (the state's anthem) helped provoke riots outside the newspaper's office.

Jay "Ding" Darling examines his Duck Stamps.

In these pages (and on our front cover), we see how Duffy's cartoons tried to warn Americans about Hitler's racism and fascism, indoctrination of German children, anti-Jewish laws, and specific episodes such as the plight of the ship *St. Louis*, which tried to bring German Jewish refugees to America.

There was Herbert Block, popularly known by his signature "Herblock," three-time Pulitzer Prize-winning editorial cartoonist for the *Washington Post* for more than 50 years. It was Block who, in a 1950 cartoon, coined the term "McCarthyism." Vice President Richard Nixon famously canceled his subscription to the *Post* after a particularly biting Herblock cartoon about him in 1954. Block's cartoons about the Holocaust drew attention to Nazi book-burnings and pogroms, as well as the obligation of the free world to help the Jews.

There was Jay "Ding" Darling, who lived a kind of double life. By day he was a two-time Pulitzer Prize-winning editorial cartoonist for the *New York Herald Tribune*; by night, he was one of America's most enthusiastic environmental activists. Darling created the Federal Duck Stamp program to protect wetland habitats and was chosen by President Franklin D. Roosevelt to head the U.S. Biological Survey (which later became the U.S. Fish and Wildlife Service). Darling's cartoons about Nazi brutality were blunt. His depiction of the Germans grinding up their victims is especially jarring, as he surely intended.

Theodor Geisel, a.k.a. Dr. Seuss.

And there was the irrepressible Theodor Seuss Geisel—better known by his pen name "Dr. Seuss"—who, before his illustrious career creating children's books, was an editorial cartoonist for the New York City newspaper *PM*. In these pages, we see how Seuss satirized the absurdity of Nazi racial theory and also created one of the most graphic cartoon depictions of Nazi mass murder.

Two of the artists whose works appear in this book were not just cartoon chroniclers of the Holocaust but were themselves very much a part of the tragic history of that era.

One was Arthur Szyk (pronounced "shick"). Szyk left his native Poland and came to the United States, settling in Connecticut in 1940. He became a leading member of the Bergson Group, a Jewish political action committee that raised public awareness of the mass murder and lobbied the U.S. government to rescue Jewish refugees. Szyk's illustrations appeared in the Bergson Group's full-page newspaper advertisements, brochures, and publications. The group called him "our one-man art department."

Arthur Szyk in his studio.

Szyk also had a strong personal reason to focus on Europe's Jews: most of his family members were trapped in German-occupied Poland. His widowed mother, age 70, was murdered in the Nazi death camp of Chelmno in 1942. "With her voluntarily went her faithful servant, the good Christian Josefa, a Polish peasant," Szyk later wrote. "Together, hand in hand, they were burned alive." Szyk's brother and many of his wife's relatives were also killed by the Nazis.

Another cartoonist whose life was intertwined with the European Jewish catastrophe was Eric Godal, who was born and raised in Germany. In the research for this book, we uncovered Godal's remarkable story of narrowly eluding a Gestapo raid in 1933. He made his way to the United States and became a political cartoonist for various publications. One of Godal's cartoons in 1938 showed a Jewish refugee labeled "The Wandering Jew" crisscrossing the globe. One year later, Godal's own mother became one of those homeless wanderers: Mrs. Anna Marien-Goldbaum and 936 other German Jewish refugees aboard a ship called the *St. Louis* were turned away from Cuba and hovered for days off the Florida coast, hoping to be granted haven in the United States.

Two heartbreaking letters "from an aged mother on the wandering steamship to her son, an artist, in New York" were published in the *New York Daily Mirror* that week. "It is so strange how near, and yet how much cut off we really are," Mrs. Goldbaum wrote. "I feel that you are backing me from far away, and that gives me courage to go on." She tried to put on a brave face: "I still have the hope that President Roosevelt and other influential people will help us…I shall not lose courage until the happy end is reached." No happy end was in sight. The president

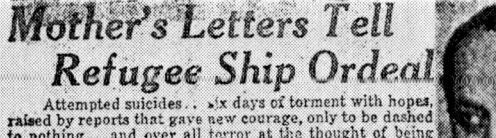
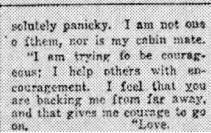

The *New York Daily Mirror* published the letters of cartoonist Godal's mother.

ignored their pleas. The *St. Louis* was forced to return to Europe. Many of the passengers, including Godal's mother, were murdered in Nazi death camps.

In 1943, Godal drew the most critical cartoon about the Roosevelt administration's policy toward European Jewry ever to appear in an American newspaper (see p.175). Now we know that in addition to his heartfelt concern about his fellow Jews in Europe, Godal also had the most compelling of personal reasons to address this subject: his own mother had been turned away from America's shores by U.S. officials like those in his cartoon.

Are the cartoons in this book now merely interesting or quaint artifacts of the past? Far from it. They illuminate a vitally important time in human history when more knowledge, sensitivity, and action could have helped save innocent people from oppression. Political cartoonists today can learn from their example, and use their craft to speak out against contemporary genocide. Some have already done so with regard to Darfur. Cartoons are powerful vehicles for teaching and learning. The images in these pages serve as a powerful reminder that prejudice and persecution can explode anywhere, at any time, and decent people have to be ready to defend everyone's civil rights and freedom. That, in the end, is why we chose to resurrect these cartoons from unseen newsprint and place them before the eye-gates of a new generation: these "damned pictures," created by cartoonists in a desperate cry against the Holocaust, can today inspire action against racism, discrimination, and persecution.

—Rafael Medoff and Craig Yoe

Kevin Kallaugher, in *The Economist*, September 25, 2004.

1. HITLER COMES TO POWER

A Nazi parade in Buckenburg, Germany, 1934.

The rise of Adolf Hitler and his National Socialists, or Nazis, to power in Germany in January 1933 caught much of the world by surprise.

As late as May 1928, the Nazis had won less than 3% of the vote in elections to the Reichstag, Germany's parliament, and the Nazi party's candidate for president received barely 1% of the votes in March 1929. But amidst Germany's spiraling economic and social chaos, the Nazis rose to 18.3% of the vote in the parliamentary election of July 1930. They doubled that total two years later, becoming the largest party in the Reichstag. Negotiations between the Nazis and other parties then produced a coalition government with Hitler as chancellor. The Nazis celebrated with a huge torchlight parade through the streets of Berlin on the night of Hitler's appointment, January 30, 1933.

A "MODERATE" HITLER?

Relatively little was known in America about Hitler, and many Americans assumed that the Nazis would not turn out to be as bad as some feared. An editorial in the *Philadelphia Evening Bulletin*, on January 30, claimed that "there have been indications of moderation" on Hitler's part. The editors of the *Cleveland Press*, on January 31, asserted that the "appointment of Hitler as German chancellor may not be such a threat to world peace as it appears at first blush." Officials of the Roosevelt administration were quoted as saying they "had faith that Hitler would act with moderation compared to the extremist agitation [i]n his recent election campaigning…[They] based this belief on past events showing that so-called 'radical' groups usually moderated, once in power."

A WAVE OF TERROR

In the weeks to follow, however, events on the ground contradicted those optimistic predictions. There were sporadic outbursts of anti-Jewish violence that were encouraged, and sometimes assisted, by the Nazi regime. In early March, for example, the *Chicago Tribune* published an eyewitness account of "bands of Nazis throughout Germany carr[ying] out wholesale raids to intimidate the opposition, particularly the Jews." Victims were "hit over the heads with blackjacks, dragged out of their homes in night clothes and otherwise molested," with many Jews "taken off to jail and put to work in a concentration camp."

The following month, the *New York Evening Post* reported that the Nazis had launched "a violent campaign of murderous agitation" against Germany's Jews: "An indeterminate number of Jews…have been killed. Hundreds of Jews have been beaten or tortured. Thousands

The Pyromaniac
Rollin Kirby
The New York World-Telegram, March 23, 1933
Another view of the Nazis' torchlight parade celebrating their rise to power.

of Jews have fled. Thousands of Jews have been, or will be deprived of their livelihood. All of Germany's 600,000 Jews are in terror."

The Hitler regime moved swiftly to begin the process of expelling the Jewish community from German society. The legal system was one of its first targets. Jews were banned from serving on juries. Jewish judges were forced out of their jobs through violence and administrative decrees. Jewish state prosecutors were compelled to retire, and the few who refused to do so were physically blocked from entering courthouses.

Jewish journalists, university professors, and orchestra conductors and musicians were likewise forced out of their jobs through threats and intimidation. On April 7, the regime enacted legislation requiring the dismissal of Jews from all government jobs. Later that month, a new law severely limited the number of Jews permitted to attend German universities, while a law passed on June 2 barred Jews from serving as dentists, and a Reich Chamber of Culture was created in September to kick Jews out of the cultural and entertainment industries.

The government also sponsored a one-day nationwide boycott of Jewish businesses, with Nazi stormtroopers stationed outside Jewish-owned stores to prevent customers from entering.[1]

HITLER'S "CHILDLIKE EYES"

Hitler's effort to improve his image abroad was helped greatly by a front-page article in the *New York Times* on July 10, 1933. The article presented the Nazi leader in sympathetic terms and provided him with a platform for long statements justifying his totalitarian policies and attacks on Jews.

"Hitler Seeks Jobs for All Germans" was the headline of the article, which was based on an interview with the Nazi leader by *Times* correspondent Anne O'Hare McCormick.

McCormick gave Hitler paragraph after paragraph to explain his actions as necessary to deal with Germany's unemployment, improve its roads, and promote national unity. The *Times* correspondent lobbed the Nazi chief softball questions such as "What character in history do you admire most, Caesar, Napoleon, or Frederick the Great?"

McCormick also described Hitler's appearance and mannerisms in a strongly positive tone: Hitler is "a rather shy and simple man, younger than one expects, more robust, taller... His eyes are almost the color of the blue larkspur in a vase behind him, curiously childlike and candid... His voice is as quiet as his black tie and his double-breasted black suit... Herr Hitler has the sensitive hand of the artist."[2]

The Watch on the Rhine
Edmund Gale
Los Angeles Times, March 30, 1933
Gale invoked one of the best-known symbols of Germany, "Watch on the Rhine," a 19th century German patriotic song exhorting the public to defend the Rhine, Germany's longest river, from the country's enemies.

Just in Case He Goosesteps Too Much!
Keith Temple
New Orleans Times-Picayune, February 4, 1933
Many in the West hoped conservative leaders in the German political and industrial sectors would restrain Hitler's radicalism.

A Good Way to Find Out
Jay Darling
New York Tribune, February 4, 1933

After the Nazis emerged as the largest party in the November 1932 elections, Germany's elderly and ailing president, Paul von Hindenburg, agreed to appoint Hitler as chancellor, the most powerful governing position in the German government. In theory, Hindenburg, as president, retained some power. Many Americans, including cartoonist Jay Darling, hoped Hindenberg would still play a major role, particularly when, as they hoped and expected, the task of governing would prove too difficult for Hitler to master.

Year One of the Second Coming of The Vandals
Carl Rose
***Jewish Daily Bulletin**,* February 4, 1934
Rose compared the Nazis to the Vandals, a notorious fifth-century Germanic tribe whose barbaric ways gave the word "vandalism" to the modern English language. The helmet alludes to the armor of medieval German warriors. With a torch in his right hand and a pistol in his left, the Nazi stands on the graves of "Truth," "Culture," "Justice," "German Judaism," and other casualties of the Hitler regime.

Four Years of the Hitler Wreckord
R. O. Berg
The Anti-Nazi Economic Bulletin, January 1937
As the single best known symbol of Nazism, the swastika appeared
frequently, and in various forms, in cartoons about Hitler and Nazi Germany.

Calvary 1933
Carl Rose
Jewish Daily Bulletin, July 23, 1933
The swastika replaces the cross, symbol of the crucifixion of Jesus at Calvary.

Calvary 1933
Rollin Kirby
New York World Telegram, September 21, 1938
Another striking use of the crucifix motif: Kirby invokes Christianity's most poignant symbol to skewer the Free World's abandonment of Czechoslovakia in 1938. (See Chapter 19).

A Throw-Back to the Dark Ages!
Edmund Gale
Los Angeles Times, April 2, 1933

2. SYMBOLS OF HATE

Most Americans knew relatively little about Hitler at the time he became chancellor of Germany in January, 1933. Although Hitler and his Nazi Party had been mentioned in U.S. newspapers on occasion in previous years, they were not regarded as likely to play a major role in Germany's future, and therefore received only slight attention in the American press. Once Hitler assumed power, however, the American public began reading and hearing a great deal about Germany's new chancellor. One of the first symbols of the new Germany with which Americans became acquainted was the stiff-armed salute.

The salute, known in German as a *Hitlergrub,* or Hitler Greeting, was actually first used by Italian fascists, around 1919, and then adopted in the 1920s by the Nazis in Germany. Embarrassed by the salute's foreign pedigree, Nazi propagandists later falsely claimed that the salute was of German origin. In the German version, it was accompanied by the words *Heil Hitler!* ("Hail, Hitler!") or *Sieg Heil!* ("Hail, victory!")

In July 1933, the Hitler salute was made compulsory for all government employees in Germany and during the singing of the German national anthem. It was known as "a bit of practical National Socialism." Failure to give the salute could result in criminal prosecution or worse. The consul-general of Portugal was once beaten by Nazi thugs for failing to salute Nazi marchers in Hamburg. Jews were prohibited from giving the salute on the grounds that their use of it would dishonor the gesture.

Another well known symbol of Nazism is the swastika. The swastika is at least 5,000 years old and derives from ancient India; in the Sanskrit language, it means "good fortune." It can be found in works of art related to a number of eastern religions, and was also used extensively by Native American tribes such as the Navajos. To this day, the swastika is still revered by many Hindus and Buddhists. Voters in Nepal choose their candidates by marking their ballots with a swastika-shaped stamp.

In the mid-1800s, German nationalists began using the swastika design, claiming it as a symbol of "Aryan" history and the "master race." By the early 1900s, it was commonly found in antisemitic publications and right wing youth movements in Germany. At the same time, it continued to appear elsewhere in Europe. For example, European aviators sometimes wore swastika medallions for good luck. Coincidentally, a school in Austria that Adolf Hitler attended as a boy had swastikas carved into the artistic designs on several of its buildings.

The Nazi Party adopted it in 1920 and Hitler himself designed the party flag, featur-

AN ADOLF HITLER ACTION FIGURE

As part of the Nazis' effort to entrench the Hitler salute in the national culture, German children were given three-inch tall plastic figurines of Hitler with a movable right arm. German housewife Helga Hartmann, who apparently did not receive the Hitler action figure, recalled how, at age five, she and a seven year-old cousin were sent by their mother to the local post office: "We went in and said *Guten Morgen* [Good Morning]. The post-office lady scowled at us and sent us back outside with the words, 'Don't come back until you've learned your manners.' We exchanged glances and didn't know what we had done wrong. My cousin thought that maybe we should have knocked. So we knocked and said *Guten Morgen* again. At that point, the post-office lady took us by the hand, led us back to the door, and showed us how, upon entering a public building, you were to salute the Fuhrer. That's my memory of 'Heil Hitler!' and it's stayed with me to this day."

The Nazi salute is today illegal in Germany, Austria, the Czech Republic, and, under certain circumstances, in Sweden.

AMERICA'S SALUTE

Francis Bellamy (1855 – 1931), an author and Baptist minister, composed the pledge of allegiance to the American flag in 1892. His associate James Upham designed an accompanying salute, which consisted of raising the right arm, palm down. The pledge and salute were gradually adopted in schools throughout the country. After the Italian fascists and the Nazis adopted a similar gesture, there was a groundswell of public support in the United States for changing America's salute. As a result, Congress in December 1942 changed the Bellamy salute, as it was known, to the gesture of placing a hand over one's heart.

ing a black swastika in a white circle against a red background, which were the colors of the flag of the pre-World War I German Empire. In his book *Mein Kampf*, Hitler asserted that the red represented "the social idea of the movement," the white stood for "the nationalist idea," and the swastika symbolized "the mission of the struggle for the victory of the Aryan man." Less than six weeks after Hitler's rise to power, the Nazi Party flag was declared a national flag alongside the old German colors.

Public display of the swastika is today illegal in Germany, Austria, Poland, Hungary, and Lithuania. In 2001, the executive commission of the European Union proposed anti-racism legislation that would have included a continent-wide ban on display of the swastika, but the final version of the bill that was passed in 2007 did not ban the swastika, because some EU member-states regarded such a prohibition as an infringement on free speech. In addition, European Hindus lobbied against the ban, arguing that the Nazis had "hijacked" their ancient religious symbol. [3]

Germany's Newest Ensign
Edmund Duffy
Baltimore Sun, March 3, 1933
Hitler declared the swastika to be the new official symbol of Nazi Germany and made it the centerpiece of the nation's flag. But Duffy had a different view as to Nazism's real flag.

We and They
Daniel R. Fitzpatrick
St. Louis Post-Dispatch, November 11, 1938
A German's hand gives the Nazi salute, symbolizing dictatorship. By contrast, an American's hand exercises the democratic right to vote, symbolizing freedom.

A Salute to the World
Edmund Duffy
Baltimore Sun, February 1, 1933
The hapless German nation is thrust into the center of international conflict by the Nazis, symbolized by the Hitler salute.

Hail Hitler
Herbert Block
NEA Syndicate, April 5, 1933
The Nazi leader receives the Hitler salute from figures representing coercion, intolerance, bigotry, and ignorance.

3. BURNING BOOKS, BURNING PEOPLE

Nazi book burning in Berlin, May 10, 1933.

Soon after rising to power, Hitler began the process of "Nazification" of Germany's elementary schools, high schools, and universities. All Jewish teachers, as well as any teachers suspected of not being pro-Nazi, were fired. Twenty past or future Nobel Prize winners were among those dismissed. Schools were prohibited from using books that the Nazis regarded as "degenerate"—meaning any books that differed from the Nazis' perspective on political, social, or cultural matters, as well as all books by Jewish authors.

The Hitler regime chose May 10, 1933 as the date for a nationwide "Action Against the Un-German Spirit," a series of public burnings of the banned books. The gatherings were organized by pro-Nazi student groups under the supervision of the Minister of Propaganda, Joseph Goebbels.

The largest of the thirty-four book-burning rallies, held in Berlin, was attended by an estimated 40,000 people. Books by German Jews such as Albert Einstein and Sigmund Freud were burned, as well as books by the British science fiction writer H.G. Wells (author of *The Time Machine* and *The War of the Worlds*) and many American writers, including Ernest Hemingway *(For Whom the Bell Tolls)*, Jack London *(Call of the Wild)*, and even Helen Keller.

"No to decadence and moral corruption!," Goebbels declared in his remarks at the rally. "Yes to decency and morality and state!...The soul of the German people can again express itself. These flames not only illuminate the final end of an old era; they also light up the new."

A *New York Times* editorial sarcastically suggested that the Nazis might next begin "burning microphones" to stamp out free speech. *Time* called the Nazis' action "a bibliocaust," and *Newsweek* described it as "a holocaust of books." This was one of the first instances in which the term "holocaust" was used in connection with the Nazis. The word "holocaust" derives from an ancient Greek word meaning a burnt offering, as in a sacrifice to a deity.

Among the authors whose books the Nazis burned was the 19th century German Jewish poet Heinrich Heine, who in one of his plays had prophetically warned, "Where they burn books, they will also one day burn people."

"JUST LETTING OFF STEAM"

Five years later, protests by American college students helped prevent another mass book-burning by the Nazis. A front-page story in the *New York Times* on April 24, 1938 revealed that the new Nazi rulers of Austria had sent the chief librarian of the world-famous Austrian National Library a list of "non-Aryan" books "to be removed and burned." Students at Williams College in Boston sent a telegram to the Austrian library offering to

HELEN KELLER AND THE NAZIS

Helen Keller (1880 – 1968) was an American author, political activist, and lecturer. She was the first deaf-blind person to earn a college degree. After the Nazi book burnings, she wrote this open letter:

To the Student Body of Germany:

History has taught you nothing if you think you can kill ideas. Tyrants have tried to do that often before, and the ideas have risen up in their might and destroyed them.

You can burn my books and the books of the best minds in Europe, but the ideas in them have seeped through a million channels, and will continue to quicken other minds. I gave all the royalties of my books to the soldiers blinded in the World War with no thought in my heart but love and compassion for the German people.

Do not imagine your barbarities to the Jews are unknown here. God sleepeth not, and He will visit his Judgement upon you. Better were it for you to have a mill-stone hung round your neck and sink into the sea than to be hated and despised of all men.

---

buy the banned books. Riots broke out on the Williams campus when anti-Nazi students tried to burn Hitler in effigy, and pro-Nazi students used fire hoses to stop them.

At Yale University, an editorial in the students' newspaper, the *Yale Daily News,* urged the school administration to purchase the Austrian books, an action which it said would both add to Yale's "intellectual equipment" and at the same time "administer a well-justified backhanded slap" at the Nazis. But Professor Andrew Keogh, Yale's chief librarian, disagreed. "I must stay clear of politics," Keogh declared, and therefore "under no circumstances would the Yale Library buy non-Aryan books" from the Austrians. Keogh said that since the Nazi regime prohibited the export of books, purchasing them would constitute "a political violation." Keogh also claimed that "European bonfires are never so serious as the newspapers would make them." He said the book-burnings in Germany were just "students letting off steam."

Nevertheless, the protests by students at Williams, Yale, and other universities appear to have had an impact: the Austrian National Library announced that the books in question would be locked away rather than burned.

"LIKE BURNING PEOPLE"

References to the Nazi book burnings have appeared frequently in American culture, sometimes in unexpected ways. In a 1976 episode of the popular television series *The Waltons,* the family's eldest son, John Boy, hears a radio report about book-burnings in Germany, and remarks, "Burning books is like burning people! Why would people do such craziness?" A local minister attempts to organize a public burning of Hitler's book *Mein Kampf* and other German-language books, which John Boy forestalls at the last moment when he points out that one of the books is a German Bible, prompting the minister to have a change of heart.

Ray Bradbury's famous science fiction novel *Fahrenheit 451* depicts a futuristic society in which all books are illegal and "firemen" armed with flamethrowers hunt them down. (The book's title refers to the temperature at which paper ignites without a match.) In his introduction, Bradbury recalled: "[W]hen Hitler burned a book I felt it as keenly, please forgive me, as his killing a human, for in the long sum of history they are one and the same flesh. Mind or body, put to the oven, it is a sinful practice, and I carried that with me."[4]

Burnt Offering
Herbert Block
NEA Syndicate, May 13, 1933
A Nazi official presents a "burnt offering," or religious sacrifice, of forbidden books to his idol, Adolf Hitler, in the manner of ancient peoples offering sacrifices to their deities.

On the Altars of the Nazis
Jacob Burck
The Daily Worker, May 11, 1933
First, they burned books; now, they burn people.

Apotheosis
Carl Rose
Jewish Daily Bulletin, April 30, 1933
An apotheosis is the elevation of a person to the level of a divine being. For Rose, the burning of the great books, and the elevation of Hitler's book *Mein Kampf (My Struggle)* to the equivalent of the Bible, constituted a kind of apotheosis by the Nazis.

M. W.

This cartoon, which originally appeared in the 1933 booklet *Hitler's Crime,* shows the Nazi leader attempting to appear as a respectable statesman as he faces the world, while he is at the same time setting fire to books behind him, out of sight.

Keeping the Home Fire Burning
Russell T. Limbach
Fight Against War and Fascism
December 1936

Joseph Goebbels warms his hands over a pile of burning books.

4. MINISTER OF HATE: JOSEPH GOEBBELS

Joseph Goebbels, 1939.

The Hitler regime implemented a government-sponsored propaganda program to inculcate the German masses with Nazi ideology. Newspapers and other publications that opposed any aspect of Nazi policy were banned. All periodicals, radio broadcasts, films, theatrical productions, and books were required to conform to Nazi philosophy.

In March 1933, Hitler appointed Joseph Goebbels as Minister of Public Enlightenment and Propaganda. A Nazi party veteran with a Ph.D. in literature, Goebbels was relentless in his determination to bring about what he called "a transformation in the worldview of our entire society, a revolution of the greatest possible extent that will leave nothing out, changing the life of our nation in every regard."

THE BIG LIE

Goebbels conceived the theory of the "big lie"—that the bigger the lie, the more likely people would believe it. Under his direction, the German government completely controlled the press, radio, and movie industry, and he made full use of them to propagate an array of wild lies about Jews, accusing them of everything from poisoning Germany's wells to using the blood of Christian children in their religious rituals. These efforts were instrumental in persuading the German public that Jews were the enemy and that Hitler was Germany's savior. The steady diet of anti-Jewish propaganda in the press and arts provided average Germans with the rationalizations and emotional commitment necessary to take part in, or at least refrain from protesting against, the Holocaust.

Goebbels also organized the Nazi regime's mass book burnings and initiated government-sponsored mob violence (pogroms).

One of the most important Nazi propagandists serving under Goebbels was Julius Streicher, editor-in-chief of *Der Stürmer (The Stormtrooper)*, the most prominent anti-Jewish publication in Nazi Germany. *Der Stürmer*, which had a weekly circulation of half a million, featured sensationalist stories intended to whip up grassroots anti-Jewish hatred. Streicher also ran a publishing house that produced antisemitic literature for children, including the popular book *Der Giftpilz (The Poisonous Mushroom)*, in which a mother teaches her son that "the Jew is the cause of misery and distress, illness, and death."

The Call to the Pogrom
Carl Rose
Jewish Daily Bulletin, May 20, 1934
Goebbels's propaganda was not merely rhetoric; it also incited hatred and violence.

"Mother, are we International Bankers?"

International Bankers
Mischa Richter
New Masses, November 14, 1939
Nazi propagandists claimed that "Jewish international bankers" secretly controlled the world's economy. Richter offered a view of that slander through a child's eyes.

The Weeping Crocodile of Franconia
Carl Rose
Jewish Daily Bulletin
May 13, 1934

Julius Streicher cries phony crocodile tears over a Jewish pogrom victim even as he sells copies of *Der Stürmer* urging readers, "Annihilate the Jews!" (Franconia is a region of Germany where Streicher was the local Nazi leader.)

"Now This is Going to Hurt Me More Than You!"
Eric Godal
PM, January 28, 1943
Goebbels gives doses of Nazi lies to the "patient," who represents the German public.

The Largest Purveyors of Their Line in the World
Carl Rose
Jewish Daily Bulletin, June 13, 1934
Goebbels and *Der Stürmer* editor Julius Streicher as the proprietors of a store selling Nazi lies.

The Gospel of a Perfect Aryan
Carl Rose
Jewish Daily Bulletin, January 17, 1934
Hitler explains the principles of Nazi propaganda. At his side is Goebbels, holding a sign reading "When Jewish blood spurts from the knife," a line from the lyrics of a popular Nazi song.

5. TEACHING CHILDREN TO HATE

Hitler viewed Germany's schools as a breeding ground for raising an entire generation of Nazis. Among his regime's first steps were to dismiss Jewish teachers from public schools and prohibit Jewish students from attending.

A NAZI VERSION OF *CINDERELLA*

The curricula in German schools were radically revised to reflect Nazi ideas and traditional textbooks were replaced with Nazi versions. Biology texts now advocated the theory of "Aryan" racial superiority. Atlases focused on the alleged danger to Germany posed by surrounding nations and the supposed theft from Germany of various territories. History books presented justifications for renewed German militarism. The Nazis even concocted their own version of the famous fairy tale *Cinderella* with the prince choosing the racially pure young heroine and rebuffing her racially alien stepmother.

German children learn hate in a Nazi classroom.

A scene from Disney's *Education for Death* cartoon.

At a press conference in September 1934, President Franklin D. Roosevelt expressed concern that the German government seemed to be preparing young people for war with Germany's neighbors, such as France. He related a story he had heard from an American tourist in Germany about an eight year-old German boy who, in his bedtime prayers each night, would say, "Dear God, please permit it that I shall die with a French bullet in my heart."[5]

DISNEY EXPOSES THE NAZIS

During World War II, Disney created a series of short cartoons to support the American war effort and expose the nature of Nazism. They were shown in movie theaters before the main feature. One especially striking nine-minute short was called *Education for Death: The Making of the Nazi*. It follows a German child, Hans, as the Nazi school system turns him into a worshipper of Hitler. When Hans's teacher shows the pupils a fox capturing and eating a rabbit, Hans makes the innocent mistake of expressing sympathy for "the poor rabbit." He is made to sit in the corner with a dunce cap, while another student gives the "correct" answer: "The world belongs to the strong....The rabbit is a coward and deserves to die."

Finally surrendering to peer pressure, Hans agrees that the rabbit was "a weakling" that got what it deserved.

The teacher then provides the moral of the story: the German people are "an unconquerable super race" who will "destroy all weak and cowardly nations." Hans's upbringing proceeds with endless "marching and 'Heil'-ing, 'Heil'-ing and marching," as he becomes almost a robot, blindly heeding the Nazi Party's orders to "trample on the rights of others." The Disney narrator concludes: "For now his education is complete—his education for death."

The intensive Nazi education that German children received in their classrooms ensured that they would fill the ranks of the Hitler Youth movement. Its membership increased from 50,000 on the eve of Hitler's election in 1933 to 5.4 million in 1936. Strong peer pressure compelled the participation of even those children who were less committed to Nazi ideology.

At age ten, boys joined the German Young People group, while girls were assigned to the League of Young Girls. At 13, boys graduated into the Hitler Youth movement, where they received paramilitary training, while girls joined the League of German Girls, where they were indoctrinated with the Nazi image of young women as the propagators of the Aryan race.

During the early years of World War II, Hitler Youth performed only auxiliary tasks for the military, but, as German losses mounted in 1943, large numbers of 16, 17, and 18 year-olds were drafted and saw battle.

HITLER YOUTH IN ACTION

Menachem Weinryb, an Auschwitz survivor forced to take part in a death march from Poland to Germany, recalled how, when they reached the Belsen area on April 13, 1945, the German guards went to a nearby town "and returned with a lot of young people from the Hitler Youth [and local policemen]....They chased us all into a large barn....we were five to six thousand people.... [They] poured out petrol and set the barn on fire. Several thousand people were burned alive."

Hitler Youth members took part in numerous atrocities, from forcing Vienna's Jews to scrub the streets with toothbrushes to the mass shooting of Jews swimming from sinking boats in the German harbor of Lubeck. In addition, many of those who graduated from Hitler Youth filled the ranks of the Gestapo and participated in the annihilation of European Jewry. While other branches of the Nazi apparatus collapsed or surrendered in the waning days of World War II, Hitler Youth remained fanatically loyal to their Fuhrer to the very end, which is why one often finds mention of them in eyewitness accounts of atrocities against Jews in the spring of 1945, during the final days of the war.

The Little Brown (Shirt) Schoolhouse
Edmund Duffy
Baltimore Sun, April 15, 1933
A classic symbol of American education, the one-room school building known as the "little red schoolhouse" was popular in rural areas in the 19th and early 20th centuries. In this cartoon, the Hitler version of the schoolhouse refers to the brown shirts that were part of the Nazi stormtroopers' uniforms.

The Patriot Master's Reward
Irwin D. Hoffman
Jewish Daily Bulletin, April 19, 1934
The teacher who bullies his students and teaches them to hate Jews is considered a true patriot in Hitler's eyes. By putting incorrect answers to the math equations on the chalkboard, the cartoonist is mocking the Nazi ideology also written there.

6. THE NAZIFICATION OF THE UNIVERSITIES

Hitler quickly transformed Germany's universities into incubators for Nazism. A nation known for centuries as the world's center of higher learning, to which students of arts and sciences flocked from around the globe, now turned higher education into a means for breeding antisemitism, racism, and militarism.

Symbolic of the Nazification of German universities was the removal of a statue of Athena, the Greek goddess of wisdom, from the entrance to the main building at the University of Heidelberg. It was replaced by a bronze eagle, representing Germany, facing west toward France, Germany's enemy. The old inscription, "To the Eternal Spirit," was replaced with the words "To the German Spirit" and a golden swastika.

German university students take part in a book-burning, 1933.

The first round of anti-Jewish legislation enacted by the Nazis, in the spring of 1933, included laws intended to bring about what the Nazis called the *Saeuberung*, or "cleansing," of Germany's universities. Jewish professors, as well as non-Jewish scholars who were deemed "politically unreliable," were barred from holding faculty positions in German universities. Non-Jewish candidates for teaching positions who had Jewish spouses were automatically disqualified from consideration.

TERRORIZING JEWISH STUDENTS

The number of Jewish students at German universities was quickly and drastically reduced through a combination of antisemitic harassment by Nazi students, cancellation of financial aid, and the imposition of a 1.5% quota for Jewish applicants.[6]

The diary of Marianne Steinberg, a 22 year-old medical student at the University of Dusseldorf when the Nazis came to power, provides a glimpse of the antisemitic terror that Jewish students faced on campus: "Our rights and duties [as students] have been taken away. We no longer belong to the German student body. According to the Fuhrer's stipulations, we here in Dusseldorf can only take our seats after all the Aryans have found their places." A merit scholarship that she had been awarded previously was soon cancelled and she was disqualified from receiving any other financial aid because of her "non-Aryan lineage." Almost penniless, Marianne was forced to travel to England to work as a maid and nanny.

EINSTEIN'S DECISION

The mass firing of Jewish professors left some universities without one-fourth to one-third of their faculties. Among the victims was the world famous physicist Albert Einstein, who had taught at the Prussian Academy of Sciences in Berlin. Einstein had been visiting the United States when Hitler came to power in January 1933. He decided not to return to Germany. "I do not desire to live in a country or belong to a country where the rights

SQUASHING DISSENT

Columbia students protesting the invitation to Nazi Germany's ambassador to speak on campus in 1933.

Columbia University students held a rally outside the mansion of university president Nicholas Murray Butler, to protest his decision to participate in the Heidelberg event.

Butler responded by expelling rally leader Robert Burke from Columbia, on the grounds that Burke had spoken "disrespectfully" about him. Burke was never readmitted, even though he had excellent grades and had been elected president of his class. Later, Columbia's own attorney acknowledged that "the evidence that Burke himself used bad language is slight."

of all citizens are not respected and where freedom of speech among teachers is not accorded," Professor Einstein explained.

All books authored by Jews, or that were in any way inconsistent with Nazi thought, were banned from Germany's universities. The government-controlled German Students' Association orchestrated a nationwide book burning campaign in May 1933. Many of the burnings took place on university campuses and were amply attended by faculty and students. More than 20,000 books were burned in a bonfire near the University of Berlin campus, before crowds estimated at 40,000 strong.

Although a small number of German professors resigned rather than serve the Nazis, most agreed to radically revise their teachings to fit the Hitler agenda. Biologists and anthropologists now taught theories of Aryan racial superiority. Law professors became advocates for the Nazi legal system. Physicists fashioned a version of physics that they said was free of any traces of "Jewish influence."

Professors of medicine became devotees of Nazi medical ideas, such as the value of euthanizing the handicapped and sterilizing people regarded as inferior. Faculty at the University of Heidelberg initiated what they called "spatial research," to advance Hitler's drive for *Lebensraum,* that is, seizing territory from Germany's neighbors as "living space" for the expanding German populace.

TEA WITH A NAZI

Some prominent American universities sought to maintain friendly relations with the Nazi regime and with Nazi-controlled German universities in the 1930s. While Williams College terminated its program of student exchanges with Nazi Germany, Columbia, Yale, Princeton, Bryn Mawr, and other U.S. colleges and universities declined to do likewise. They refused to change their policy even after a German official candidly asserted that his country's students were being sent abroad to serve as "political soldiers of the Reich."

In 1933, Columbia president Nicholas Murray Butler invited Nazi Germany's ambassador to the United States, Hans Luther, to speak on campus. In 1936, Columbia and more than 20 other American universities took part in the 550th anniversary celebration of the University of Heidelberg even though Heidelberg had been purged of Jewish faculty members, instituted a Nazi curriculum, and hosted a burning of Jewish-authored books. Professor Arthur Remy, who served as Columbia's delegate to the Heidelberg event, later remarked that the reception at which Nazi Propaganda Minister Josef Goebbels presided was "very enjoyable."

Harvard University president James Conant welcomed Hitler's foreign press spokesman, Ernst "Putzi" Hanfstaengl, to campus in 1934. Hanfstaengl, a Harvard alumnus, took part in the 1934 Harvard commencement and had tea at Conant's home. Conant sent an official Harvard delegate to the 1936 Heidelberg celebration. He also invited Nazi academics to Harvard's 1936 tercentenary celebration, prompting Albert Einstein to boycott the event.

Heidelberg
Ad F. Reinhardt
The Student Advocate, April 1936
Hitler extends a friendly invitation to the Heidelberg event—while sitting on top of a cannon and burning books.

Unlike some American university presidents, Conant refused to offer faculty positions to European Jewish refugee scholars to shield them from persecution. Moreover, when an official of the DuPont corporation privately asked Conant, a chemist, for his advice about hiring the German Jewish refugee scientist Max Bergmann (who was later described by the *New York Times* as "one of the leading organic chemists in the world"), Conant urged him not to hire Bergmann, deriding him as "very definitely of the Jewish type—very heavy."[7]

Post-Graduate Work for German Professors
Carl Rose
Jewish Daily Bulletin, May 7, 1933
German university professors are sent back to school, as students, for "post-graduate work" under Nazi supervision: they are compelled to study Hitler's beliefs and revere them as something akin to the Bible, as the students read "The Gospel According to Saint Adolf."

7. HITLER ON TRIAL

American Jewish organizations looked for ways to expose the nature of Nazism and keep the plight of German Jewry in the public spotlight. On the first anniversary of Hitler's rise to power, the American Jewish Congress held a mock trial of Hitler before "the High Court of Humanity," at Madison Square Garden in New York City. Highlighting the broad range of opposition to Nazism among Americans, the trial was cosponsored by the American Federation of Labor, the American Civil Liberties Union, Actors Equity, and other nonsectarian groups.

News coverage of the trial.

The event was called "The Case of Civilization Against Hitlerism." It was structured along the lines of a criminal case, with former Secretary of State Bainbridge Colby serving as presiding judge and prominent attorney Samuel Seabury as the prosecutor. The Nazi German ambassador to the United States, Hans Luther, was invited to appear as defense attorney for Hitler. The German government protested that the invitation was an insult and Secretary of State Cordell Hull, anxious to preserve friendly U.S. relations with Berlin, assured the Nazis that he "frowned upon" the invitation and was "disappointed" that he could not stop the trial from taking place.

Prominent individuals from various walks of life appeared as prosecution witnesses, each making a presentation summarizing Hitler's offenses against a particular group. For example, New York University president Harry Woodburn Chase spoke on behalf of the academic community; Dr. Lewellys Barker, professor of medicine at Johns Hopkins University, addressed Hitler's exploitation of the German medical profession; and novelist Stanley High spoke about the mistreatment of writers in Nazi Germany. New York City Mayor Fiorello La Guardia and U.S. Senator Millard Tydings (D-Maryland) appeared on behalf of "American public opinion."

THE VERDICT

The event concluded with Nazi Germany being found guilty of having "turned its face against historic progress and the positive blessings and achievements of modern civilization." Only one of the 21 specific points listed in the indictment referred to Germany's Jews. The emphasis was on Hitler's suppression of civil rights and democracy in general.

The mock trial of Adolf Hitler and Nazi Germany achieved its main purpose. The proceedings were broadcast live on leading New York City radio stations, and were reported widely in the American press, thus helping to further enlighten the public as to the true nature of the Nazi regime.

The Indictment
Carl Rose
Jewish Daily Bulletin, March 9, 1934
A figure representing the civilized world indicts Adolf Hitler.

8. RACISM AS A WAY OF LIFE

The ideological foundation of Nazism was a racial theory which claimed that Germans and other northern Europeans were members of an "Aryan" race that was biologically superior to all other races. Adolf Hitler's close associate Alfred Rosenberg, the chief ideologue for the Nazi Party, developed this idea from the writings of 19th-century racist and nationalist philosophers.

Rosenberg was particularly influenced by Arthur de Gobineau, author of the influential 1853 book *Essay on the Inequality of the Human Races,* and popularizer of the term "Aryan." According to de Gobineau, the world is divided into three races—white, black, and yellow—and mixing between them is to blame for many of mankind's problems.

Blending the writings of de Gobineau, other racial theorists, and Hitler's personal opinions, Rosenberg produced an ideology that shaped Nazi Germany's domestic and foreign policy. Since Jews were regarded as the root of all evil and racially unassimilable, they had to be completely segregated from German society and then either driven out or killed. Germans were the "master race" and destined to rule the world. Scandinavians were racially close to Germans and could be assimilated into Germanic society.

Alfred Rosenberg on trial for war crimes at Nuremberg, 1946, flanked by a courtroom security guard.

On the other hand, Poles, Slavs, and other East Europeans, while not on the same level as Jews, were the by-products of racial mixing and could never ascend to the level of Aryans. Their role was to be subjugated and to serve Germany. Asians and Arabs, although racially inferior to Aryans, could be military allies.

Eventually, in the Nuremberg Laws of 1935 (see Chapter 10), the Nazis would codify their racial criteria, defining a Jew as someone who had at least one Jewish grandparent.

"ARYAN" PHYSICS

In their obsessive drive to bring about the complete separation of German Jews from the rest of German society, the Nazis insisted that all contributions by Jews to German culture and science were tainted. The works of Jewish playwrights, novelists, musicians, and artists were declared "degenerate" and banned. Books by Jewish authors were burned.

The Nazis also attempted to promote "Aryan physics" as a counter to the prominence of Jewish scientists, such as Albert Einstein, in the world of physics. Similar efforts were undertaken to delegitimize Jewish contributions in mathematics, chemistry, biology, and other fields.

"What is the prisoner's crime, comrade?"
"Crime? He's worse than a criminal! They say his grandfather was a Rabbi!"

Nazi Concentration Camp
Carl Rose
Jewish Daily Bulletin, June 11, 1933
Even a helpless infant was considered an enemy and worthy of imprisonment, if he had Jewish relatives.

Nazis Ban Tuberculin for Cattle Because its Discoverer is a Jew
Carl Rose
Jewish Daily Bulletin, March 6, 1934
Rose took aim at the absurd lengths to which the Nazis went to avoid being "contaminated" by contact with anything Jewish. He was responding to reports of a Nazi ban on the work of the German Jewish biologist Robert Koch, whose findings concerning tuberculosis (discovered through experiments on cattle) earned him a Nobel Prize in 1905.

Can These Restrictions Have Been Overlooked by Unser [Our] *Adolf?*
Carl Rose
Jewish Daily Bulletin, May 8, 1934

Mein Early Kampf
Dr. Seuss
PM, January 21, 1942
Mocking Hitler's obsessive hatred of anything with a seeming Jewish connection, Theodor Seuss Geisel, better known as Dr. Seuss, depicted baby Hitler refusing milk from Holstein cows because of their presumably Jewish-sounding name. The cartoon's title parodies the title of Hitler's book, *Mein Kampf ("My Struggle")*.

Masterpieces
Will B. Johnstone
New York World Telegram, December 1936
In 1936, the Nazis banned literary and theatrical criticism, ordering all commentary on the arts to adhere to Nazi racist philosophy. In this parody of the new Nazi culture, books by Jewish authors such as Lion Feuchtwanger are thrown in the trash, plays by Jewish playwrights such as Ernst Toller are declared off-limits, and music by Jewish composers such as Felix Mendelssohn may not be played.

9. THE COLD POGROM

The word *pogrom*, derived from a Russian verb meaning to wreak havoc or to destroy, came into vogue in connection with anti-Jewish riots in Czarist Russia in the late 1800s and early 1900s. It usually refers to mob attacks that are sponsored or encouraged by the government.

Immediately upon Adolf Hitler's rise to power, in January 1933, there were scattered outbreaks of anti-Jewish violence, which were approved, but not necessarily organized by, the new government. The Hitler regime's strategy for action against its Jewish citizens during those first months was based not on mob assaults, but on enacting laws to severely limit the ability of Jews to work in various professions. The Nazis hoped such restrictions would make life unbearable for German Jews and drive them out of the country. Jews were banned from the civil service and many Jewish lawyers and doctors were dismissed from their jobs. Another law, enacted in May, banned Jews from owning land or engaging in agricultural pursuits. Even kosher butchers were outlawed. In addition, the Nazi regime organized a nationwide one-day boycott of Jewish businesses on April 1, 1933.

German Jewish refugee Max L. Berges authored the novel *Cold Pogrom* in 1939, to dramatize the economic persecution of the Jews under Hitler.

ECONOMIC STRANGULATION

As early as April 18, 1933, a news article in the *New York Times* about the Jews in Germany used the phrase "cold pogrom," which it explained as "the economic strangulation enforced by the Nazis against the German Jews." The author and journalist James Waterman Wise, in his 1933 book *Swastika: The Nazi Terror,* defined a "cold pogrom" as "economic annihilation and moral degradation, effected through legal measure and without physical violence."

Journalist Dorothy Thompson explained the Nazi regime's mindset this way: "Obviously it is impossible to assassinate half a million Jews in cold blood, and therefore the cold pogrom is undertaken which forces them to leave Germany by closing down one by one opportunities to earn a living or educate their children beyond the elementary grades, and by social ostracism." Thompson wrote a three-part series for the *Jewish Daily Bulletin* in May 1933, in which she made prominent reference to the concept of a cold pogrom.[8]

Victims of Cold Pogrom Need Your Aid—Give!
Carl Rose
Jewish Daily Bulletin, June 25, 1933
Rose appeals to readers to contribute to the relief of Jews being persecuted in Germany.

One Despot to Another
Carl Rose
Jewish Daily Bulletin,
October 8, 1933

Nero, leader of the ancient Roman Empire, is notorious for having burned down most of the city of Rome to clear space for the building of his palace. Here he contrasts his use of fire with Hitler's method of "cold" pogroms.

Nero: "In my days, Adolf, I never thought of Cold Pogroms."

The Sower
Edmund Duffy
Baltimore Sun
May 13, 1933

Early on, the Nazis banned Jews from agricultural work. Referring to the Biblical verse, "They who sow the wind, reap the whirlwind" (*Hosea* 8:7), this cartoon predicted that, by sowing anti-Jewish hatred through such laws, the Nazis would reap bad fortune.

59

Untitled
Fred Ellis
The Daily Worker
April 1933

Jews in Europe played an important role in many aspects of European culture, including art, literature, music, and science. Ellis points to the fact that the Nazi laws excluding Jewish participation in society would deal a terrible blow to European culture.

10. THE NUREMBERG LAWS

A scene from the Nazi Party assembly in Nuremberg in 1935, at which broad new anti-Jewish laws were decreed.

At the annual Nazi Party congress in Nuremberg on September 15, 1935, the Nazi leadership issued a series of laws and regulations that stripped German Jews of their citizenship, denied them the right to vote or hold office, banned social relations between Jews and non-Jews, and enshrined in German law the concept that having at least one Jewish grandparent defined an individual as a Jew.

Even a Jew who converted to Christianity was still regarded by the Nazis as a Jew; the law was based strictly on racial criteria. The Nuremberg Laws provided the legal basis for the persecution of German Jews and cast them out of German society. This represented an important turning point in the events leading up to the Holocaust.

GERMANY'S NEW FLAG

The significance of the anti-Jewish decrees issued at Nuremberg at first were not widely understood. As a result, a minor additional law adopted at Nuremberg, proclaiming the swastika to be Germany's official symbol and making it the centerpiece of the German flag, attracted more attention in the American press than the other legislation. A report in the *Los Angeles Times,* for example, was headlined "Defiance to Jews of Entire World Hurled by Hitler," with the subheadlines "Swastika Made Sole German Flag by Special Reichstag Session" and "Citizenship Limited." *Newsweek* headlined its story "Hitler Decrees Reich Flag," with the subheadings "Bars Intermarriage" and "Relegates Jews to Dark Ages."

Swastika Over Germany
Daniel Fitzpatrick
St. Louis Post-Dispatch, September 17, 1935
A bent and chained person forms the swastika on this version of the new German flag.

The Official Flag on the Old Staff
Edmund Duffy
Baltimore Sun, September 17, 1935
Note the contrast between this cartoon and Duffy's March 1933 cartoon of Hitler holding a flag, on p.25. He drew the first cartoon at a time when Hitler had just risen to power, and it was not yet completely clear what policies the Nazi leader would pursue. Thus the earlier figure of Hitler is more cartoonish and less menacing, and the flag is mounted on an ordinary pole. But by the time of this cartoon, in September 1935, it was clear that Hitler was engaged in violent and systematic oppression of the Jews. Hence this depiction of Hitler is much more threatening, and he holds a spiked club rather than a flagpole.

The New Ten Commandments
Myles Pergament
The Anti-Nazi Bulletin, January 1939

While the Nuremberg Laws established the rules and regulations the Nazis followed to eliminate Jews from German society, this cartoon used the Ten Commandments to satirically portray the laws the Nazis were really following. This cartoon's reference to "Jews and Catholics" as both being Hitler's victims, like the depiction (on p.20) of "The Church" being crushed by Hitler alongside the Jews, reflects two perceptions among some people in the West: that Hitler was persecuting Christians as well as Jews, and that the American public would be more sympathetic to the plight of the Jews if it recognized that the Nazis were a danger to everyone, not just Jews. About 98% of the German population was Christian. The vast majority of German Protestants, and most German Catholics as well, either supported, or did not voice opposition to, the policies of the Hitler regime. On some occasions, the Nazis acted against specific churches or clergymen, especially Catholics, whom they regarded as troublemakers. In addition, Christians who had at least one Jewish grandparent were regarded as Jewish and persecuted accordingly. But there was no systematic policy of persecuting Christians or churches in general.

11. DOING BUSINESS WITH HITLER

During the 1930s, the Roosevelt administration strove to maintain normal trade relations between the United States and Nazi Germany. Jewish organizations and other groups disagreed with this policy. They urged Americans to refrain from purchasing German-made products as a protest against Hitler's persecution of German Jews. Jewish activists frequently picketed stores that carried goods manufactured in Germany.

New York City mayor Fiorello La Guardia was an outspoken opponent of U.S. trade relations with the Nazis. In 1935, the city's Bridge Authority purchased five hundred tons of sheet steel from Germany to build what is today known as the Triborough Bridge, connecting Manhattan, Queens, and the Bronx. Although bedridden at Mount Sinai Hospital, the feisty mayor swung into action when he heard about the steel contract.

IMPORTING HATRED

In a telegram to Bridge Authority chairman Nathan Burkan, the mayor announced that he did not want that "damned steel" in his city. "The only commodity we can import from Hitlerland now is hatred," La Guardia declared, "and we don't want any [in] our country."

Technically, the Bridge Authority was an independent agency that did not require the mayor's approval for its construction purchases, but Mayor La Guardia found grounds to block the deal: he bore responsibility for New Yorkers' safety, and could not vouch for the reliability of Hitler's steel. He wrote to Burkan: "I cannot be certain of its safety unless I first have every bit and piece of German-made material tested before used. *Verstehen Sie* [Do you understand]?"

La Guardia took his share of heat for his protests against Nazi Germany. Six thousand German-Americans held an anti-La Guardia rally, at which they pledged to vote him out of office. Nazi propaganda chief Joseph Goebbels threatened to bomb New York City. Secretary of State Cordell Hull complained that La Guardia's actions were harming German-American relations. The mayor was not fazed. "I run the subways and he runs the State Department—except when I abrogate a treaty or something," he declared in classic La Guardia style.[9]

THE MAYOR AND THE MASSEUR

In 1935, a German citizen residing in New York City named Paul Kless applied for a masseur's license. The city's License Commissioner was prepared to approve the application, in accordance with the U.S.-German Treaty of Friendship. But Mayor La Guardia overruled the Commissioner and rejected the application on the grounds that "it is well known that American citizens of the Jewish faith have been discriminated against in Germany." If the Germans were not abiding by the treaty, then he saw no reason to abide by it, either.

Fiorello La Guardia

A Little Lesson in Economics
Carl Rose
Jewish Daily Bulletin, July 30, 1933
Media reports in the summer of 1933 linked a decline in Nazi Germany's exports around the world to the impact of a boycott of German products organized by American Jewish protesters. This cartoon makes the same connection, pointedly placing senior Nazi official Hermann Goering and Propaganda Minister Joseph Goebbels, the two figures most prominently associated with anti-Jewish violence, alongside Hitler as they watch the export figures decrease.

A Qualified Valentine
John Cassell
Brooklyn Eagle, February 14, 1939
In early 1939, there were rumors that some countries might curtail their trade with Germany in response to the persecution of the Jews. Some news media reports suggested that the Germans might be willing to ease their attacks on the Jews in order to preserve trade relations with the West. Hence John Cassell, on Valentine's Day, portrayed Hitler as a suitor trying to woo "World Trade" with "A Qualified Valentine"—offering to be "pretty good to the Jews," ominously adding "for a while..."

How Much Will You Pay Me to Stop?
Keith Temple
New Orleans Times-Picayune, March 30, 1939
A Nazi brute tries to extort economic concessions from the figure on the right who represents the international community.

12. ARYANIZATION

One of the actions taken by the Nazis in the 1930s to restrict Jewish participation in German society was what they called "Aryanization." This involved the forced sale of Jewish property to non-Jews at a small fraction of its value, and the forced replacement of Jewish owners of businesses by non-Jews.

A major step in this process was an edict issued on April 26, 1938, restricting the access of Jews to their bank accounts and requiring Jews to report many of their private assets to the government. The German Ministry of the Interior subsequently set the value of Jewish companies at levels far below their actual worth, then pressured the owners to sell them to non-Jews. These actions left many Jews almost penniless.

THEN THEY CAME FOR HER BICYCLE

Similar measures were adopted in countries that the Germans occupied. Hungary, for example, was taken over by the Nazis on March 19, 1944. Ten days later, legislation requiring the registration and Aryanization of Jewish property, including even bicycles, was enacted. Eva Heyman, a 13 year-old Hungarian Jewish girl, wrote in her diary on April 7:

"Today they came for my bicycle....[It] had a proper license plate, and Grandpa paid the tax for it. That's how the policemen found it, because it was registered at City Hall that I have a bicycle....So, dear diary, I threw myself on the ground, held on to the back wheel of my bicycle, and shouted all sorts of things at the policemen: 'Shame on you for taking away a bicycle from a little girl! That's robbery.' We had saved up a year and a half to buy the bicycle....I went to the store and took the bicycle home, only I didn't ride it but led it along with my hands, the way you handle a big, beautiful dog. From the outside I admired the bicycle, and even gave it a name: 'Friday.' I took the name from *Robinson Crusoe*, but it suits the bicycle. First of all, because I brought it home on a Friday, and also because Friday [the character in the book] is the symbol of loyalty, because he was so loyal to Robinson....

Eva Heyman, 1944.

"One of the policemen was very annoyed and said: 'All we need is for a Jewgirl to put on such a comedy when her bicycle is taken away. No Jewkid is entitled to keep a bicycle anymore. The Jews aren't entitled to bread either; they shouldn't guzzle everything, but leave food for the soldiers.' You can imagine, dear diary, how I felt when they were saying this to my face. I had only heard that sort of thing on the radio, or read it in a German newspaper. Still, it's different when you read something and when it's thrown in your face. Especially if it's when they're taking my bicycle away."[10]

Birds of a Feather
Rollin Kirby
New York World Telegram, November 21, 1938

Simplified Finance
Herbert Block
NEA Syndicate
May 5, 1938
Hermann Goering, who at this point was in charge of Nazi Germany's economic affairs, demands money from a figure labeled "Juden," German for "Jews." The cartoonist portrays robbing the Jews as Germany's simplified method of dealing with financial matters.

Shakedown
Bruce Russell
Los Angeles Times, April 29, 1938
A "shakedown," the slang term for criminals pressuring their victims to give them money, is invoked here to show a giant Nazi literally shaking his Jewish victim in order to get his money.

No Regard for the Misery
Ainsworth H. "Doc" Rankin
Brooklyn Eagle, May 2, 1938

13. THE LEAGUE OF NATIONS

Established in the aftermath of World War I, the League of Nations was envisioned by its sponsors as a means of promoting disarmament and resolving international conflicts, so as to prevent another world war. It did not live up to its hopes in those areas, but the League's High Commissioner for Refugees, Dr. Fridtjof Nansen of Norway, was generally successful in resettling large numbers of Europeans who had been displaced by the war.

A session of the League of Nations in 1935.

In May 1933, European and American Jewish organizations submitted a petition to the League on behalf of Franz Bernheim, a German Jewish resident of the Upper Silesia region bordering Poland. Bernheim, who lost his job because of German laws against hiring Jews, argued that such anti-Jewish discrimination in Silesia violated a post-World War I German-Polish treaty concerning the treatment of minorities in that territory. The League upheld Bernheim's complaint. The Hitler regime, which at that point was anxious to avoid international sanctions, refrained from imposing anti-Jewish laws in that small area for the next several years. This episode gave many American Jews hope that the League of Nations would help protect Germany's Jews.

Meanwhile, to address the spiralling German Jewish refugee problem following Hitler's rise to power, the League in October 1933 created a new department, the High Commission for Refugees Coming from Germany. An American political scientist, James G. McDonald, was selected as Commissioner.

McDonald soon found himself challenged by a variety of obstacles. Hitler complained that the establishment of the new High Commission constituted interference by the League of Nations in Germany's internal affairs. The League responded by making McDonald's office completely independent. One consequence was that member nations of the League felt no responsibility to contribute financially to the operations of the High Commission. Nearly all of McDonald's funding was provided by private Jewish organizations and it was not sufficient. McDonald asked President Franklin Roosevelt for a small U.S. contribution in order to encourage other countries to donate funds. FDR promised $10,000, but never followed through on his pledge.

ROOSEVELT'S DISAPPOINTING RESPONSE

The most serious problem McDonald encountered was that, as the worldwide depression deepened in the mid-1930s, numerous countries tightened their restrictions against immigration. McDonald's search for a haven where large numbers of German Jews could be resettled was unsuccessful. He was particularly disappointed by the response of President Roosevelt, who praised and encouraged McDonald's work but would not take concrete steps to assist the refugees. After two years, McDonald resigned in protest against the international community's failure to cooperate with him in addressing the plight of German Jewry.

The hope that the League of Nations would come to German Jewry's defense was further eroded by developments in the mid and late 1930s. Because the League's ruling council required a unanimous vote to enact a resolution, serious action could never be taken if even one of the major powers objected. Moreover, the League had no military force of its own, so its decisions could be implemented only if its member-nations had the will to enforce them.

Britain and France, the League's leading powers (the U.S. and the Soviet Union were not members), preferred to appease fascist nations rather than challenge their aggressive actions, such as Germany's rearmament, Japan's invasion of China, and Italy's conquest of Ethiopia. As a result, the League was unable to organize meaningful responses to those developments. This seriously eroded the League's credibility and left it virtually helpless to defuse mounting international tensions. Refugee advocates soon realized that German Jews could expect little real help from the League of Nations.

S.
Opinion
November 1933

Reflecting some Americans' optimistic expectations, a winged figure, representing the League of Nations, shields oppressed German Jewry from a Nazi attacker.

14. THE NAZI OLYMPICS

Track star Jesse Owens.

As the summer of 1936 approached, Hitler and the Nazis prepared to exploit their most significant propaganda opportunity yet: the Olympics.

Back in 1931, two years before the Nazis rose to power, the International Olympic Committee (IOC) awarded the 1936 Olympic games to Germany. After Hitler became chancellor in 1933, anti-Nazi activists in the United States began arguing that Nazi Germany's policies should disqualify Berlin from hosting the games. They pointed out that the exclusion of Jews from German athletic organizations and denying Jews access to government-funded training facilities contravened the IOC's requirements of equal treatment for all competitors.

To counter such criticism, the Nazis permitted fencer Helene Mayer, who was of partial Jewish descent but did not consider herself Jewish, to return from exile and serve on the German Olympic team. Ironically, Mayer had fled Germany in 1933 because of the regime's discrimination against those who were categorized as "Mischling," that is, "mixed race." Mayer ended up winning a silver medal at the Berlin games. On the winners' stand, she wore a swastika armband and gave the Hitler salute.

Hitler also invited a German Jewish high jumper, Margaret Lambert, to take part in the try-outs. That gave ammunition to supporters of U.S. participation, such as American Olympic Committee president Avery Brundage. Visiting Germany to inspect preparations for the games, he claimed that Jewish athletes were being allowed to train adequately in separate, privately-funded facilities.

Lambert's try-out jump of 1.60 meters tied the German high-jump record, but just days before the games opened, she was informed by the authorities that she did not make the team because of her "mediocre performance." The Germans did not even have three women high jumpers to field, as did other Olympic teams. One of their two jumpers later turned out to be a man who disguised himself as a woman on orders from Nazi officials. Ironically, the Hungarian athlete who won the high-jump in the 1936 games reached the same height Lambert did in the try-outs, 1.60.

ATHLETES WITH A CONSCIENCE

During the months preceding the 1936 games, many prominent Americans called for boycotting the Olympics to protest the Nazis' persecution of German Jewry. The July 1935 pogrom against Jews in Berlin, and the promulgation of the anti-Jewish Nuremberg Laws two months later, increased U.S. public opposition to the games. In addition to American Jewish organizations, groups such as the National Association for the Advancement of Colored People (NAACP) and the Catholic War Veterans also endorsed the boycott.

A number of American Jewish athletes refused to go to Berlin, including championship jumper Syd Koff, who had won four gold medals at the 1932 Maccabean Games in Tel Aviv and had qualified for the 1936 team. Star sprinter Herman Neugass, of Tulane University, wrote to a New Orleans newspaper: "It's my unequivocal opinion nobody should go because of the way Jews are treated." Harvard track and field stars Norman Cahners and Milton Green also boycotted the games, as did speed skater Jack Shea, a Catholic who had won a gold medal in the 1932 games.

HITLER'S OLYMPIC FRIEND

Avery Brundage, president of the American Olympic Committee, strongly supported American participation in the Berlin games. He dismissively described the plight of Jews in Germany as "the present Jew-Nazi altercation." He claimed that opposition to U.S. participation in the Nazi Olympics was "a Jewish-Communist conspiracy" to "make the American athlete a martyr to a cause not his own." Even afterwards, Brundage insisted that the games contributed to "international peace and harmony."

Avery Brundage

Brundage's attempt to organize a track and field meet between the U.S. and Nazi Germany in 1939 was unsuccessful. Explaining his failure to a German colleague, Brundage wrote that "because of the overwhelming proportion of Jewish advertising, our papers have been filled with anti-Nazi propaganda." It later emerged that after the Olympics, Brundage asked the Nazis to award his construction company a contract to build a new German Embassy in Washington. His request was accepted, but the onset of World War II foiled the project.

The Long Island University Blackbirds basketball team was widely regarded as the top team in the country. Its players —some of whom were Jewish and some not— voted unanimously to boycott the Olympics to protest the Nazis' persecution of German Jews. Their action stunned the sports world. One prominent sports columnist, Frank Eck, chastised the Blackbirds for causing "ill feelings" by bringing the German Jewish issue into the discussion.

The Amateur Athletic Union, which certified American athletes to compete in the Olympics, debated the issue at its December 1935 convention. It resolved —by just two and a half votes—to endorse America's participation.

NAZI "HOSPITALITY"

Shortly before foreign visitors began arriving in the summer of 1936, antisemitic literature was taken off the newsstands in Berlin. Physical assaults on Jews were kept to a minimum during the games. Visiting journalists were impressed. The *New York Times* praised the German government for its "flawless hospitality." A *Los Angeles Times* correspondent wrote: "Zeus, in his golden days, never witnessed a show as grand as this." An editorial in that newspaper even predicted that the "spirit of the Olympiads" would "save the world from another purge of blood."

Many Americans derived satisfaction from the fact that an African-American track star, Jesse Owens, won four gold medals in the Berlin games. Some observers believed Owens's success undermined Hitler's claims of Aryan racial superiority. Two of Owens's Jewish teammates, Marty Glickman and Sam Stoller, were removed from the competition at the last minute; the coaches feared the Nazis would be offended if Jewish athletes took part.

The Berlin Olympics gave Hitler a way to soften his public image and allay the international community's concerns about his bigotry, violence, and militarism. Even President Roosevelt was taken in, at least to some extent. He told American Jewish leaders how impressed he was to learn from two tourists who attended the games "that the synagogues are crowded and apparently there is nothing very wrong in the situation [of Germany's Jews] at present."

Olympic Games
William Gropper
Fight Against War and Fascism, November 1935

The Modern Mercury
Jerry Doyle
Philadelphia Record, December 7, 1935
The figure in silhouette is Mercury, a god from ancient Roman mythology. The wings on his feet, helmet, and staff allude to his remarkable speed. Because of his running ability, Mercury is used here to symbolize the noble ideals of Olympic competition; the cartoon shows him racing against Hitler, who carries a torch—another Olympic symbol—that burns flames labeled "intolerance and discrimination." In artistic depictions of Mercury throughout history, and in this cartoon as well, he is shown carrying a staff, known as a caduceus, which consists of wings and two intertwined snakes. Hitler, by contrast, is shown carrying a staff topped by a swastika and featuring one snake, labeled "Nazism."

Hitlerite Sportsmanship
Carl Rose
Jewish Daily Bulletin, July 16, 1933
Hitler, Goebbels, and Goering are clad in the garb of ancient Greece, where the Olympic competition was created, as they review a display of Nazi "sportsmanship."

"We're doing nothing to prevent him from entering Olympics."

Carl Rose
Jewish Daily Bulletin, November 26, 1933

15. NAZISM SPREADS

The rise of Nazism in Germany strengthened pro-Nazi movements elsewhere in Europe in the 1930s, and encouraged some governments to enact antisemitic legislation and tolerate attacks on their Jewish citizens. Germany's Jews were no longer the only European Jewish community under assault.

In Romania, for example, the two largest antisemitic political parties, the National Peasants Party and the League of National Christian Defense, united in late 1937 and established a coalition government. Although the new regime lasted less than two months, it held power long enough to enact legislation that stripped one-third of Romania's 750,000 Jews of their civil rights. These efforts paved the way for additional anti-Jewish discrimination and legislation by subsequent Romanian governments, and further encouraged the rising tide of popular antisemitism in the country.

Antisemitic graffiti defacing a synagogue in the northern Italian city of Trieste, 1938.

MUSSOLINI AND THE JEWS

Benito Mussolini and his Fascist Party, the rulers of Italy since 1922, did not mistreat the country's small Jewish population during their first years in power. In the mid-1930s, however, Mussolini drew increasingly close to Hitler and began to turn against Italy's Jews. In the autumn of 1938, he issued a series of racial laws that stripped Jews of their civil rights, prohibited them from studying or teaching in public schools, banned marriage between Jews and non-Jews, ejected Jews from a wide range of professions, and expelled thousands of foreign-born Jews from the country altogether.

When Slovakia became an independent state in early 1939, following the German annexation of the other parts of the former Czechoslovakia, antisemitic policies were quickly implemented. Father Josef Tiso, the new ruler, approved of the increasing outbursts of violence and looting against Slovakian Jews and oversaw the forced relocation of many Jews to the no-man's-land along the Slovakian-Hungarian border. The Tiso regime, which signed a friendship treaty with Hitler as one of its first acts in office, enacted a slew of anti-Jewish regulations, including the Aryanization (seizure) of Jewish property and Nuremberg-style laws excluding Jews from social and economic life.

Extreme rightist Karlis Ulmanis, who came to power in a coup in Lithuania in 1934, facilitated a brand of strident Lithuanian nationalism that led to a harsh deterioration in the economic lives of the country's Jewish citizens. In the name of "Lithuaniazation," the regime severely reduced the number of Jews in government jobs, helped push Jews out of various private industries, and fostered an environment of economic pressure that significantly decreased the number of Jewish students enrolled in Lithuanian universities. This atmosphere, together with sporadic instances of localized anti-Jewish violence,

> ### GHETTO BENCHES
>
> One of the most blatant forms of anti-Jewish harassment in Poland in the 1930s was the institution of segregated seating for Jewish students in some Polish universities. At the Lwow Polytechnicum, starting in 1935, and later at Warsaw Polytechnic and most other Polish institutions of higher learning, Jews were forced to sit in the back of classrooms in an area known as the "ghetto benches." If there were insufficient seats there, the Jewish students were made to stand, even if there were empty seats elsewhere in the room. Students who ignored the regulation were often assaulted and students who boycotted classes as a protest were severely penalized. The Polish Ministry of Education at first opposed the practice on the grounds that it violated the treaties Poland signed after World War I to protect ethnic minorities. But, under pressure from antisemitic student organizations, the ministry ruled in 1937 that individual universities had the right to decide their own seating policies.
>
> **U. S. WRITERS SEND PROTEST TO POLAND**
> Condemn 'Ghetto Benches' in Universities, See Threat to Nation's Culture
>
> *Headline of a New York Times article on Americans protesting against "ghetto benches" in Poland in 1937.*

made life tenuous for many Jews in interwar Lithuania.

QUOTAS, PRESSURE, DISCRIMINATION

In Poland, longstanding grassroots antisemitism combined with the calamitous impact of the worldwide depression made life increasingly intolerable for the country's 3.3-million Jews during the 1930s. In the wake of World War I, Poland had signed "minorities treaties" that were supposed to protect Jews as well as other ethnic minorities. Nevertheless, antisemitic discrimination and occasional violence became the norm in Poland in the years leading up to World War II.

Local anti-Jewish boycotts were also common in interwar Poland. Gangs of antisemitic thugs confronted Christian artisans, shopkeepers, and landlords and pressured them to refrain from doing business with Jews. Those who cooperated with the boycott were given signs to put in their windows declaring that they dealt only with "Aryans." Those who refused had their names published in extreme nationalist newspapers. The boycott enforcers also routinely carried out physical assaults on Jewish businesses, demanding that they close down. These attacks often escalated into all-out pogroms. A study of Jewish-owned stores in 11 towns in Poland's Bialystok region found that, from 1932 to 1937, the number of Jewish shops decreased by more than one-third. The Polish government endorsed anti-Jewish boycotts as necessary to bring about the "Polonization" of the nation's economy, which, they claimed, was under Jewish control.

Antisemitism took longer to gain ground in interwar Hungary than in some other parts of Europe during the 1930s, but there too it grew steadily, especially in the Hungarian armed forces. The "First Jewish Law," as it was known, was adopted by the parliament in May 1938. It set a maximum quota of 20% for Jews in numerous professions and economic enterprises. The "Second Jewish Law," enacted in May 1939, reduced that number to just 5% and defined Jews in racial terms, so that it applied even to Jews who had long ago converted to Christianity. The Hungarian government in 1939 also created Jewish forced-labor brigades, into which tens of thousands of Jewish men were drafted to dig ditches, clear forests, and build roads.

Fresh Fields
Edmund Duffy
Baltimore Sun, January 2, 1938

The Swastika Spur
Edmund Duffy
Baltimore Sun, September 2, 1938
Since Italy is known for the boot-like shape of its southern borders, this cartoon uses the swastika as the boot's spur, symbolizing the enactment of Nazi-style laws by the Mussolini government against Italy's Jews.

16. HITLER'S MOVE INTO AUSTRIA

Adolf Hitler had long dreamed of making his native Austria part of neighboring Germany. In the very first paragraph of his autobiography, *Mein Kampf*, he wrote that the "reunion" of Austria and Germany *(Anschluss,* in German) is "a task to be furthered with every means our lives long." He argued that since the two countries were ethnically similar and had been associated in the past, it was Germany's destiny to absorb Austria.

In early 1934, as Austrian chancellor Engelbert Dollfuss was weighing possible changes to the Austrian constitution, Hitler stepped up his pressure on the Austrians to embrace the ways of Nazism. When Dollfuss rejected Hitler's overtures, Austrian Nazis assassinated him. Their attempted coup failed, however, and the plotters fled to Germany. There, with Hitler's support, they staged terrorist attacks on Austrian government institutions. These provocations increased civil turmoil in Austria and helped pave the way for German military intervention.

> **22 SUICIDES IN ONE FAMILY**
>
> Three generations—22 members—of a single Jewish family in Vienna, the Wolkners, took their own lives in response to the *Anschluss*.
>
> The last of the suicides, 18 year-old Gertrude, a musician, left a note asking that a single marker be placed over the graves of all her family members.
>
> *Nazis force Jews to scrub the streets of Vienna, March 1938.*

AN ORGY OF SADISM

In March 1938, German troops marched into Austria to impose the *Anschluss* and were greeted by huge, cheering crowds. Violent antisemitism erupted almost immediately in the capital city of Vienna, home to most of Austria's 190,000 Jewish citizens. The world-famous psychologist Dr. Sigmund Freud, a resident of Vienna, wrote to a friend: "The people in their worship of antisemitism are entirely at one with their brothers in the Reich."

"There was an orgy of sadism," reported famed CBS Radio broadcaster William L. Shirer, who was on the scene, but had to fly to London to elude Nazi censorship in reporting the news of the *Anschluss* and its aftermath. [14]

Shirer wrote: "Day after day large numbers of Jewish men and women could be seen scrubbing [slogans supporting ousted anti-Nazi chancellor Kurt Schuschnigg] off the sidewalk and cleaning the gutters. While they worked on their hands and knees with jeering stormtroopers standing over them, crowds gathered to taunt them. Hundreds of Jews, men and women, were picked off the streets and put to work cleaning public latrines and the toilets of the barracks where [Nazi secret police officers] were quartered. Tens of thousands more were jailed. Their worldly possessions were confiscated or stolen."

The suicide rate among Vienna Jews skyrocketed in the weeks following the *Anschluss*. At the same time, the lines outside the U.S. consulate in Vienna stretched for blocks, as tens of thousands

Dr. Sigmund Freud

of Austrian Jews sought permission to immigrate to America. According to U.S. law, a maximum of just 1,143 Austrian citizens could be admitted annually.

For most Americans, the persecution of Jews in Europe was a remote subject. It was something that was happening far away, to strangers with whom they had little in common. Only in rare instances was one of the victims sufficiently well known that a significant number of Americans recognized him. Sigmund Freud was one of those exceptions.

Dr. Freud, the founder of the field of psychoanalysis (a term he coined in 1896), was the best known psychologist in the world and probably the only Austrian Jew well known to the American public. Notice that when Edmund Duffy drew his cartoon (p.92) about the German takeover of Austria, his list of Nazi outrages had "Dr. Freud Arrested" ahead of "Religious Intimidation" and "Continued Persecution of Minorities." Duffy assumed that the average *Baltimore Sun* reader was likely to recognize Freud's name.

INFERIORITY COMPLEX

The concept of an "inferiority complex" was developed by one of Freud's early collaborators, Alfred Adler, and often associated with Freud—hence the sarcastic suggestion, in the title of Duffy's cartoon, that Nazi abuses were the product of an inferiority complex among Germany's leaders.

Freud was deeply rooted in Vienna, where he headed the influential Vienna Psychoanalytic Society, lectured at the University of Vienna, and saw patients about whom he published a number of important studies.

Although distressed by the rise of the Nazis in neighboring Germany, Dr. Freud did not regard them as a serious threat and showed no interest in leaving his native Austria. When his books were included in the 1933 German book burnings, he remarked, "What progress we are making. In the Middle Ages they would have burned me. Now, they are content with burning my books."

Even after the German annexation of Austria in March 1938, Freud initially resisted emigrating, despite the urging of his colleagues. News reports suggesting that Dr. Freud was arrested by the Nazis—prompting Duffy's cartoon—were incorrect. However, his apartment was twice raided by the Nazis and his daughter, Dr. Anna Freud, was briefly detained and interrogated by the Gestapo. Anna's arrest convinced him to leave. On June 4, Freud, his wife Martha, and his daughter Anna fled to Paris, then London, where Dr. Freud passed away the following year.

Advice From Hitler's Special Ambassador
Carl Rose
Jewish Daily Bulletin, March 4, 1934
Austrian chancellor Engelbert Dollfuss is lectured by Hitler's "ambassador" of antisemitism.

Anschluss
Carl Rose
Jewish Daily Bulletin, May 1, 1934
Agitation by pro-Nazi Austrians in the early 1930s for *Anschluss*, or unification with Germany, was mocked by Carl Rose. He suggested that the "unity" they had in mind would consist of little more than Austrian Nazis mimicking German Nazi hatred of Jews. "Perish the Jew" *(Juda Verrecke,* in German) was a popular Nazi slogan.

Next?
Cecil Jensen
Chicago Daily News, March 20, 1938
In the wake of the *Anschluss*, Cecil Jensen depicted Austria as a woman brutalized by a German caveman, repeating the common misperception that Austria was an unwilling target of German aggression. The caveman consults Hitler's book, *Mein Kampf,* to choose his next victim.

All Our Lessons to Do Over Again
Jay Darling
New York Tribune, March 27, 1938
Some cartoonists viewed the *Anschluss* as part of a broader problem of dictators using force to get their way.

Does He Really Like It?
Keith Temple
New Orleans Times-Picayune, March 27, 1938
A hapless Austrian is chained by Nazi restrictions. Many Americans found it difficult to believe that the Austrians sincerely embraced the Nazi way of life. In fact, Austrian popular support for the *Anschluss* was enthusiastic and widespread.

Inferiority Complex
Edmund Duffy
Baltimore Sun, March 27, 1938
With his foot crushing the Austrian capital of Vienna, the figure representing Nazi Germany holds a list of examples of what the Nazi presence has introduced to Austria: the arrest of world-famous psychiatrist Sigmund Freud (actually he was not arrested, but the Nazis did raid his apartment and detain his daughter); and "religious intimidation" and "continued persecution of minorities," referring to the mistreatment of Austria's Jews. The title of the cartoon refers to a psychological condition that features prominently in Freud's writings.

17. PAPER WALLS

Beginning in 1921, immigration to the United States was governed by a system of strict quotas based on national origin. The quota for Germany was 25,957, meaning that a maximum of 25,957 German citizens could immigrate to the U.S. each year. The quota for Austrian nationals was 1,143 annually. Soon after the *Anschluss*, the Roosevelt administration announced it would combine the Austrian immigration quota with the quota for Germany. In theory, the merger of the two would benefit the terrorized Jews of Austria, who would be eligible to receive unused places in the German allotment.

The lucky ones: European Jewish immigrants arriving at New York City's Ellis Island.

That was in theory. In practice, however, it was another story. The reason there were unused places in the German quota was because American consular officials in Europe went above and beyond the law to find excuses to reject applicants for visas. They imposed numerous extra regulations, which have been described by the noted historian David S. Wyman as "paper walls." These requirements made it very difficult for refugees to qualify for admission. The Roosevelt administration was determined to keep the number of Jewish refugees entering the United States as low as possible.

A German or Austrian Jew applying for a visa to the U.S. had to present more than 50 pages of documents proving that he or she had no criminal record and no significant health problems, as well as a detailed financial statement from someone in the United States who would guarantee that the immigrant would not become a "public charge" (that is, dependent upon the government for assistance). Most German Jews did not have friends or relatives in the U.S. to provide such guarantees.

Those who did have distant relatives sometimes found that was not sufficient to satisfy the consuls. President Roosevelt himself asserted in 1936 that a distant relation might feel "no legal or moral obligation to support the applicant," if push came to shove.

If the applicant was missing just one document, the consular officials would usually reject him. For example, if someone presented a document showing he was married in a Jewish religious ceremony, but was unable to obtain a copy of his civil marriage certificate from a German government office, consul officials usually regarded his children as "illegitimate." That was enough to disqualify him.

Dr. Moritz Herzberg, a German Jewish physician, applied to the U.S. consulate in Berlin for a visa with a financial guarantee from the American Friends Service Committee, an American Quaker group that aided refugees. The consul rejected the application on the grounds that the guarantee had to come from an individual, not an organization. Herzberg eventually located a cousin in New York City who provided the guarantee. The consul rejected it on the grounds that in one part of the application, the cousin stated he earned $40 per week while on another page, he wrote that his property was worth $40—essentially, a typo.

> **ONE MORE TRAGEDY**
>
> Miss Liesel Wolfe, 37, of Munich, reached the United States in April 1938 on a six-week visitor's visa. Such a visa was much easier to obtain than permission to immigrate, but it also gave the visitor only a very brief period to meet the immigration requirements. Liesel searched desperately to find someone to provide a financial guarantee for her. Had she succeeded, she still would have had to leave the United States temporarily—perhaps going to Canada or Mexico—and apply for an immigration visa from outside the country, waiting there for months, maybe even years. In any event, Liesel was unable to find a guarantor. The night before her visitor's visa expired, Liesel, despondent at the prospect of being forced to return to Nazi Germany, jumped to her death from the fifth floor of the Clara de Hirsch Home for Working Girls, in New York City, where she had been living.
>
> **ENDS LIFE TO ESCAPE RETURN TO GERMANY**
>
> Jewish Woman Had Failed to Win Right to Remain Here
>
> Faced with the prospect of returning to Germany because she had failed to certify that she would not become a public charge, Luise

The fact that German and Austrian Jews were refugees fleeing from Nazism did not result in any special consideration for visas. The Roosevelt administration did not recognize "refugee" as a special category, because it feared that such a designation would be insulting to the Hitler regime.

In 1933, only about 5% of the German quota places were filled. The numbers rose gradually in the years to follow, but as late as 1938, the quota was still only 65% full, and in all of the years of Hitler's reign (1933-1945), it was filled only once. Even the tiny Austrian quota itself was never filled between 1933 and 1938. Thus, while the quota system certainly was a significant obstacle to Jewish refugee immigration, the way in which U.S. officials administered the system made the problem much worse.

U.S. immigration policy reflected the attitude and wishes of President Roosevelt. He believed that neither Asian nor Jewish immigrants could easily or quickly become loyal Americans. In a series of articles he authored in the 1920s, FDR characterized Asians as "non-assimilable," urged severe restrictions on admitting them to the United States, and warned against marrying Asians on the grounds that "the mingling of white with oriental blood on an extensive scale is harmful to our future citizenship..." Roosevelt was likewise unsympathetic to the idea of admitting significant numbers of Jewish immigrants. According to the diary of Vice President Henry Wallace, FDR once remarked that "the best way to settle the Jewish question...is to spread the Jews thin all over the world."

FDR's vision of America was one in which the country had to "digest" only a small number of such foreigners. The extremely tight immigration procedures that prevailed during his years in office (1933-1945) were consistent with the kind of America he seemed to prefer. [15]

The Wandering Jew
Eric Godal
Ken, April 7, 1938
The original myth of the "Wandering Jew," dating back to the 13th century, alleges that one Jew who was present at the crucifixion, and who supposedly either mocked or struck Jesus, was condemned to wander the earth for all eternity as a punishment. The haggard and bent figure, often with a sack over his shoulder and clutching a walking stick, has appeared in numerous poems, paintings, plays and folktales over the centuries, even in the works of such mainstream authors as Rudyard Kipling and Nathaniel Hawthorne. This cartoon presents the mythical Wandering Jew of old in a new and all too real form, as the Jews of Germany, Poland, Romania, and Austria are forced to leave their native lands and wander the globe, in search of a country that will take them in.

Exodus, 1938
Daniel Fitzpatrick
St. Louis Post-Dispatch, April 3, 1938
This cartoon alludes to the fact that some news reports in 1938 claimed Secretary of State Cordell Hull was preparing a plan to facilitate mass Jewish emigration from Germany. However, no such plan ever materialized. This cartoon was published shortly before the Passover holiday, which may explain his title, "Exodus, 1938." Fitzpatrick was comparing the ancient Jewish exodus from Egypt (which is commemorated by Passover) with the idea of a modern Jewish exodus from Germany.

18. A REFUGEE CONFERENCE THAT ABANDONED THE REFUGEES

The plight of Austria's Jews in the aftermath of the *Anschluss* generated pressure from some members of Congress and journalists for U.S. intervention. State Department officials decided to "get out in front and attempt to guide" the pressure before it got out of hand, as one official put it. On March 24, 1938, President Roosevelt announced that the United States was inviting 33 countries to send representatives to a conference on the refugee problem, to be held in the French resort town of Evian-les-Bains. All of those invited, except Italy, agreed to send delegates.

U.S. representative Myron Taylor addresses the Evian conference.

FDR emphasized in his announcement that "no nation would be expected or asked to receive a greater number of emigrants than is permitted by its existing legislation." In addition, the Roosevelt administration privately promised Great Britain that British-controlled Palestine would not be discussed as a possible refuge. (The British feared that admitting more Jews to Palestine would anger the Arab world.) These conditions greatly reduced the possibility that the Evian conference would produce meaningful results.

PLEASURE CRUISES BY THE LAKE

Shortly before the conference, Assistant Secretary of State George Messersmith bluntly told a private meeting of refugee advocates that the delegates to Evian were likely "to render lip service to the idea of aiding the refugees accompanied by an unwillingness, however, to do anything to ease existing restrictions on the admission of immigrants."

The Evian conference opened at the Hotel Royal on July 6, 1938. Although the delegates all arrived on time, some of the early sessions were sparsely attended. The hotel's chief concierge later recalled why: "All the delegates had a nice time. They took pleasure cruises on the lake. They gambled at night at the casino. They took mineral baths and massages at the Etablissement Thermal. Some of them took the excursion to Chamonix to go summer skiing. Some went riding; we have, you know, some of the finest stables in France. But, of course, it is difficult to sit indoors hearing speeches when all the pleasures that Evian offers are outside."

The proceedings of the conference confirmed the skeptics' fears. One speaker after another reaffirmed their countries' unwillingness to accept more Jews. Typical was the Australian delegate, who bluntly asserted that "as we have no real racial problem, we are not desirous of importing one." The only exception was the tiny Dominican Republic, which declared it would accept as many as 100,000 Jewish refugees. (That project never materialized, because the Roosevelt administration feared the arrival of so many refugees in the nearby Caribbean would enable some of them to sneak into the United States.)

SLAMMING THE DOORS

Newsweek magazine, noting the appeal by the chairman of the U.S. delegation to the attendees "to act promptly" in addressing the refugee problem, commented: "Most governments represented acted promptly by slamming their doors against Jewish refugees." *Time* magazine, for its part, reported that Evian was the source of "still and unexciting table water [and] after a week of many warm words of idealism [and] few practical suggestions," the conference "took on some of the same characteristics."

Golda Meir, who later became prime minister of Israel, attended Evian as an observer. She concluded that "nothing was accomplished at Evian except phraseology." At a press conference after the gathering, she remarked, "There is only one thing I hope to see before I die, and that is that my people should not need expressions of sympathy any more." Another critic pointed out that "Evian" was "naive" spelled backwards. The problem, however, was not naiveté so much as it was calculated indifference.

In 1979, the United States spearheaded an international conference at Lake Geneva, near Evian, on the plight of hundreds of thousands of refugees fleeing the Communist victory in Southeast Asia. In an emotional keynote speech, Vice President Walter Mondale compared the gathering to the Evian conference of 1938, which he said "failed the test of civilization." Mondale pleaded with the delegates to join the U.S. in rescuing the Asian 'boat people'. "History will not forgive us if we fail," he concluded. "History will not forget us if we succeed." The speech is widely credited with inspiring many countries to take part in the rescue of those refugees. "The nations stepped up to the crisis," Mondale's chief speechwriter, Martin Kaplan, later recalled. "It was one of those rare occasions when words may actually have saved lives." [16]

Will the Evian Conference Guide Him to Freedom?
Sidney Strube
***New York Times**,* July 3, 1938
Although the refugee bears the vague label "Non-Aryan," his beard and yarmulke indicate clearly that he is Jewish. (For more information about cartoonists using euphemisms such as "Non-Aryan" instead of "Jewish," see p.177.)

19. APPEASING HITLER

British Prime Minister Neville Chamberlain (left), architect of the policy of appeasing the Nazis, meets with Adolf Hitler in 1938.

During the 1930s, about 3 million ethnic Germans resided in Czechoslovakia, mostly in a western region near the German-Czech border known as Sudetenland (named after the area's Sudety Mountains). These Sudeten Germans comprised 23% of the Czech population.

Nationalist sentiment had always been strong among the Sudeten Germans, and it intensified in the 1920s. Sudetens complained of discrimination and protested the government's use of the Czech language in heavily-German areas, as well as its expropriation of private land for border security purposes.

The rise of Hitler to power in Germany in 1933 led to the rapid growth of a local Nazi party in the Sudetenland. When the Czech government banned the Sudeten Nazis, a new ultra-nationalist party, the Sudeten German Party, or SdP, replaced it and agitated for the secession of the Sudetenland from Czechoslovakia. Many of the protests were violent.

PRETEXT FOR AN INVASION

The SdP's activity, which was financed by the Nazi regime, was part of Hitler's strategy to provoke a crisis that could be used as a pretext for Germany to invade Czechoslovakia. At the same time, the German news media began publishing wildly exaggerated accounts of the Czech authorities supposedly persecuting Sudeten Germans.

Hitler brought matters to a boiling point in mid-September 1938. The SdP launched a wave of mob violence, including attacks on local Jews. The Czech police suppressed the riots and the SdP leaders fled to Germany. But instead of confronting Hitler, Czechoslovakia's presumed allies, Britain and France, urged Czech president Eduard Benes to make concessions.

In late September, with Hitler threatening to intervene, the British and French governments increased their pressure on the Czechs to make territorial concessions to the Nazis in order to avoid a war with Germany. British and French leaders, meeting with Hitler in Munich, Germany, on September 29-30, agreed that all Czech regions whose population was more than half ethnic German should be transferred to Germany. The Czechs reluctantly gave in and the German army moved into those territories.

Less than six months later, the Germans took over the rest of Czechoslovakia. The West did not respond.

"Villain!"
Jerry Doyle
Philadelphia Daily News, September 27, 1938
Hitler brutalizes Austria, Czechoslovakia, and Jews while pointing an accusing finger at Czech president Eduard Benes (who is watching from the window). Hitler charges Benes with mistreating the Sudeten Germans.

"As Ye Would That Men Should Do to You"
Grover Page
Louisville Courier-Journal, September 11, 1938
Page suggests that the Nazis had no right to complain about alleged mistreatment of Sudeten Germans in Czechoslovakia, in view of their own persecution of German Jews. The title of the cartoon is derived from the Biblical saying (known as the Golden Rule), "Do unto others as you would have them do unto you," which appears in the Hebrew Bible in *Leviticus* 19:18, and in the New Testament in *Luke* 6:31.

Great Sportsmen
Jay Darling
New York Tribune, September 27, 1938
As Hitler takes aim at "Defenseless Minorities," he is accompanied by his Axis partners, Benito Mussolini of Italy and Emperor Hirohito of Japan, who were likewise known for their persecution of minorities under their control. (The unflattering racial stereotypes in this depiction of the Japanese leader, and in the cartoon on page 181, were unfortunately commonplace in that era.)

C.E.D.
The Anti-Nazi Bulletin, April 1939
Vultures representing the Nazis, disregarding human rights and their treaty obligations, feast on Czechoslovakia and the Memel territory, a region that Lithuania surrendered to Germany in early 1939 after Hitler threatened to invade.

Inconsistent
George White
Tampa Tribune, September 18, 1938
The quotation comes from a speech delivered by Hitler to a Nazi Party congress on September 12, 1938. The cartoon points to the hypocrisy of Hitler complaining about the alleged persecution of Sudeten Germans, while he himself carries out the persecution of German Jews.

20. KRISTALLNACHT: SHATTERED GLASS —AND SHATTERED LIVES

On November 7, 1938, a Polish Jewish teenager distraught over his family's brutal expulsion from Germany walked into the German Embassy in Paris and shot a diplomat. The Nazi leadership used the incident as a pretext to carry out a nationwide pogrom that they had long planned.

Throughout the night of November 9-10, organized mobs of Nazi stormtroopers unleashed a hurricane of violence and destruction upon the Jews of Germany and Austria. Hundreds of Jews were beaten in the streets, and more than 90 were murdered. About 30,000 more were dragged off to concentration camps. Several hundred synagogues were burned to the ground, while fire fighters stood by, under orders from the Hitler government to act only to keep fires from spreading to property owned by non-Jews. An estimated 7,000 Jewish businesses were ransacked.

Jewish store windows smashed on Kristallnacht.

The widespread smashing of windows of Jewish homes and shops throughout Germany gave the pogrom its nickname: *Kristallnacht*, German for "Night of the Glass." It was estimated that the amount of glass broken that night equaled half of the annual amount produced by the plate-glass factories of neighboring Belgium, from which it was imported.

Afterwards, the Hitler regime imposed a fine of $1 billion Reichsmarks ($401 million) on the German Jewish community as "reparations" for the shooting of the diplomat in Paris. The government also canceled all insurance payments to German Jews whose property was damaged, forcing them to pay for all repairs themselves.

"KILL THE JEWS!"

"We heard a commotion from the street and, when we looked outside, we saw a mob of Hitler Youth [the Nazi youth movement] shouting 'Kill the Jews!' and charging towards the entrance to our apartment building," Thea Press, then 11 years old, later recalled: "My father and my grandfather grabbed a heavy broom and shoved it through the inside of the door handle. I was hiding, terrified, under a table. I remember watching the door as it creaked and bent under the pressure from the crowd. But it didn't give way."

Laurie Lowenthal, another child survivor of Kristallnacht, later described what happened to some of her relatives that night: "My father's cousin [and business partner], Ludwig Lowenthal, lived on the first floor of our house with his family. Two men broke down their front door and shot him point blank while he was in bed....His brother-in-law, Alfons Vogel, was kidnapped, taken to the nearby woods, tied to a tree and used as target practice and killed." [17]

The Nation Followed its Healthy Instincts
Edmund Duffy
Baltimore Sun, November 13, 1938
In the wake of the pogrom, Nazi Propaganda Minister Joseph Goebbels declared that the violence was an example of the German nation "following its healthy instincts."

1215–1938 and All That
Edmund Duffy
Baltimore Sun
November 18, 1938

Just as cartoonists use the character of Uncle Sam to represent the United States, they have sometimes used this character, known as Diedrich Knickerbocker, to symbolize New York State. (The 19th-century writer Washington Irving invented Knickerbocker to serve as the narrator in some of his stories, including "Rip Van Winkle.") This cartoon by Edmund Duffy was published at a time when New Yorkers were beginning to prepare for the 1939 World's Fair, which was going to be held in New York City. The British government had announced that its pavilion at the fair would include a display of the Magna Carta, the first modern document granting rights to individual citizens. Thus Duffy's cartoon shows Knickerbocker troubled by the contrast between the hopes for freedom, as symbolized by the Magna Carta, and the tragic reality reported in the headline of the newspaper at Knickerbocker's feet: "Violence and Hatred Spread Over Europe—Jews Killed."

Back to the Dark Ages
Charles Sykes
Philadelphia Evening Ledger
November 12, 1938

In this cartoon, Hitler appears in Medieval-style clothing to symbolize the era to which Nazi violence is dragging Germany.

107

And This is the Twentieth Century!
Fred O. Seibel
Richmond Times Dispatch
November 16, 1938

Meet Our New Epoch
Jay Darling
New York Herald Tribune
November 17, 1938

The "globe head" figure often appears in editorial cartoons as a symbol of the international community. Here he represents "Our Nice Little World," hearkening back to an earlier time when "Law," "Peace," "Humanitarianism," "Social Justice," and "Idealism"—the titles of the books—were the norm. But he drops the books in surprise, as he is confronted by the menacing bully, "The New Era" who uses force or threats to take what he wants. This cartoon appeared just days after the Kristallnacht pogrom. The cartoonist regarded the violence in Germany not as an aberration, but rather as typical of the harsh new era.

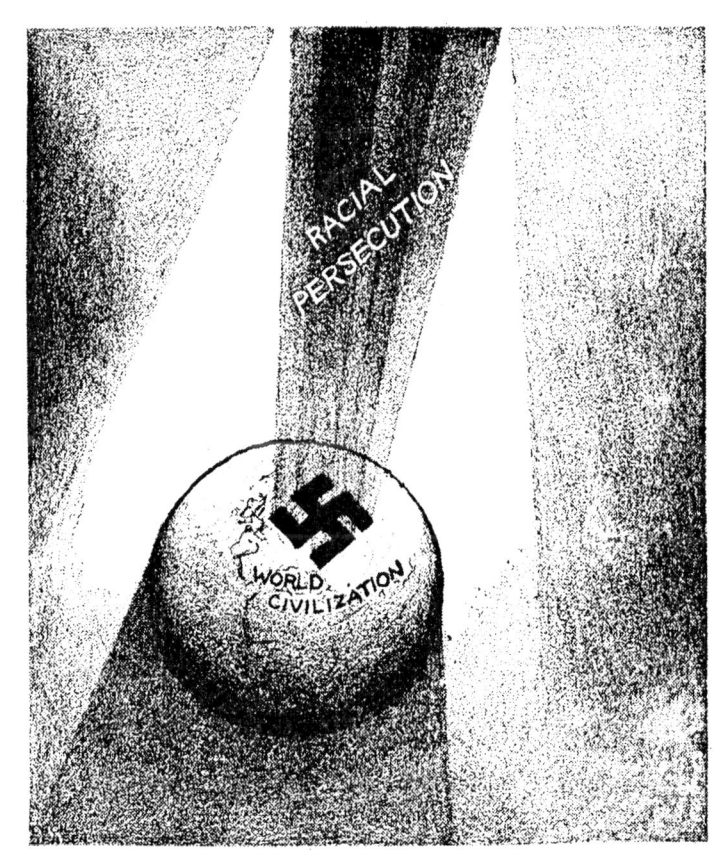

Eclipse
Cecil Jensen
Chicago Daily News
November 14, 1938

The imagery of an eclipse is used because a partial solar eclipse was due to take place one week after this cartoon was published.

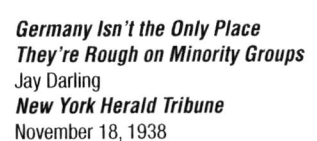

Germany Isn't the Only Place They're Rough on Minority Groups
Jay Darling
New York Herald Tribune
November 18, 1938

In an unusual twist, this cartoon compares labor activists' treatment of the American business community to the Nazis' treatment of the Jews. The reference to fines of $16 billion levied against U.S. businesses is intended to parallel the Nazis' imposition of an enormous fine on the German Jewish community to repair damage caused in the Kristallnacht pogrom.

"Go Ahead—Shoot!"
Grover Page
Louisville Courier-Journal
November 20, 1938

My Battle
Henry Elderman
Washington Post
November 13, 1938

The cartoon's title alludes to the title of Hitler's book, *Mein Kampf*, which is usually translated as "My Struggle" or "My Battle."

"Light! More Light!"
Herbert Block
NEA Syndicate
November 17, 1938

The title of this cartoon is a quote from the final words of the famous German author and poet, Johann Wolfgang von Goethe (1749 – 1832). Historians believe Goethe's call for "Light! More light!" was probably just a request to his nurse to let more light into his room, but, over the years, many have chosen to interpret those words as a plea for a more enlightened world. This cartoon portrays the candle of "German civilization" being snuffed out by Nazism; cartoonist Herbert Block's title, "Light! More light!," is a plea for more enlightened attitudes in Germany.

The Secretary of the Treasury Reports
Keith Temple
Philadelphia Inquirer
November 19, 1938

Darkness Descends
Hugh Hutton
Philadelphia Inquirer
November 14, 1938

It's None of Your Business What I Do
Hugh Hutton
Philadelphia Inquirer
November 17, 1938

This cartoon points to the international consequences of Nazi Germany's persecution of the Jews. The title, "It's None of Your Business What I Do," refers to the response of German leaders when foreign leaders criticized their mistreatment of the Jews. But in the cartoonist's view, since that persecution was driving large numbers of Jews out of Germany, it was a having direct effect on other countries.

21. THE WORLD'S RESPONSE TO KRISTALLNACHT

World statesmen criticized the Hitler regime for perpetrating the November 1938 Kristallnacht pogrom. But none of those other countries took punitive steps in response, such as severing diplomatic relations with Nazi Germany or imposing economic sanctions.

President Franklin Roosevelt condemned the violence and temporarily recalled the U.S. ambassador from Germany, Hugh Wilson, for "consultations." But the president rejected suggestions by some members of Congress to break diplomatic ties with Hitler. FDR extended the visitor's visas of approximately 12,000 German Jewish refugees who were then in the United States, but he also announced that any liberalization of America's tight immigration system was "not in contemplation." Great Britain, by contrast, agreed to admit 10,000 German Jewish children (the project was called the *Kindertransport)*, as well as 14,000 young German Jewish women who would work as housekeepers and nannies.

Shattered glass from Jewish shops on a German street.

THE WORLD LOOKED AWAY

The international community's cautious response to Kristallnacht continued a pattern that began when Hitler first rose to power five years earlier, in 1933. Other governments occasionally expressed verbal disapproval of his anti-Jewish policies, but took no diplomatic or economic action against Germany.

Likewise there had been no meaningful opposition by the free world to Hitler's aggressive military actions and violations of the Versailles peace treaty signed after World War I. While the world looked away, he expanded the German army, occupied the demilitarized border zone known as the Rhineland (1936), intervened in support of the fascists in the Spanish civil war (1936-1939), annexed Austria (March 1938), dismembered Czechoslovakia (September 1938), and pressured Lithuania to surrender the Memel region (March 1939).

European countries were loath to anger Hitler, fearing they might become his next target. Other nations, grappling with the impact of the worldwide depression, felt they could not afford to devote attention or resources to foreign problems at a time when they themselves suffered from high unemployment and other economic crises. Anti-immigration sentiment, sometimes stoked by antisemitism, made it difficult for humanitarian impulses to gain traction.

Hugh Hutton
Philadelphia Inquirer, November 16, 1938
The approach of "European Diplomacy"—giving Hitler territories such as the Sudetenland (see Chapter 19) to appease him—did not work.

Still No Solution
Herbert Block
NEA Syndicate
January 25, 1939

Humanity Mobilizes
Paul Carmack
Christian Science Monitor
November 23, 1938

Responding to news reports that a number of governments intended to aid the Jewish refugees, this cartoon optimistically portrayed the international community uniting to take action. Those hopes were soon dashed.

Beggar on Horseback
Charles Sykes
Philadelphia Evening Ledger
November 15, 1938

The proverb to which the title alludes, "Set a beggar on horseback, and he will ride to the devil," dates back to the 16th century. It means that if someone who is inexperienced or undeserving is given power, he will abuse it. As Hitler, cast in the role of the beggar, charges forward riding "anti-Semitism," the international community, labeled "Civilization," flees rather than confront the Nazi leader. The robe and sandals, garb commonly associated with ancient Rome or Greece, are used to symbolize the civilized world since those societies were known as bastions of wisdom and culture.

The Boomerang Boy
Charles Sykes
Philadelphia Evening Ledger
November 16, 1938

Hitler taking aim at a bird, which in this case is an eagle—a popular symbol of America—representing "U.S. Opinion." The swastika Hitler is about to throw is labeled "Insolence & Bluff," referring to the German leader's threatening speeches and violence such as Kristallnacht. The title of the cartoon indicates that the swastika-shaped object in his hand is in fact a boomerang, meaning that hitting the bird will come back to harm Hitler, because his behavior is alienating the American public.

Coming Home with Him!
Bruce Russell
Los Angeles Times
November 16, 1938

In response to the Kristallnacht pogrom, President Roosevelt temporarily recalled U.S. ambassador Hugh Wilson from Germany for consultations. The cartoon depicts Wilson's return as evidence of a major change in America's attitude toward Germany, with "U.S. Good Will" returning home along with the ambassador.

Civilization Can Do Better
Herbert Block
NEA Syndicate
November 19, 1938

Some cartoonists were disappointed that the international community did not respond more forcefully to the anti-Jewish violence in Germany. In this cartoon, the hand, representing the nations of the world, not only points an accusing finger at the Nazis but also reaches out to help the oppressed Jews.

**No Place to Lay
Their Heads**
Daniel Fitzpatrick
St. Louis Post-Dispatch
November 11, 1938

Verboten is the German word for "forbidden."

**The Best Answer to
Race Persecution**
Paul Carmack
Christian Science Monitor
November 16, 1938

22. KRISTALLNACHT AND CHRISTIANITY

Some American political cartoons believed that Christians had a religious obligation to respond to Kristallnacht, as the cartoons in this chapter demonstrate.

Many church leaders did condemn the pogrom, but their words of condemnation were not usually accompanied by calls for action. Not many clergymen or Christian organizations advocated opening American's doors to Jewish refugees or cutting U.S. relations with Nazi Germany.

The liberal Catholic publication *Commonweal* called for suspending America's immigration quotas in order to admit more refugees. The larger Catholic weekly magazine *America*, however, took a different line. *America* headlined its post-Kristallnacht issue "Nazi Crisis." But the two feature stories did not focus on the plight of Hitler's Jewish victims. The first was a report about the mistreatment of nuns by Nazis in Austria. The second article charged that protests by American Jews against the Nazi pogrom were generating "a fit of national hysteria" intended "to prepare us for war with Germany."

The smashed windows of a German Jewish store.

The issue did include an editorial titled "The Refugees and Ourselves," arguing that it was the "grave duty" of American Catholics to help Europe's refugees. But the editorial referred only to Catholic refugees; Jewish refugees were not even mentioned.

An editorial in the leading Protestant magazine, *Christian Century*, did address the Jewish refugee problem: it argued that America's own economic problems necessitated "that instead of inviting further complications by relaxing our immigration laws, these laws be maintained or even further tightened." It also claimed that "admitting Jewish immigrants would only exacerbate America's Jewish problem."

One notable Christian response to Kristallnacht was an initiative by the U.S. branch of the Young Women's Christian Association (YWCA). Less than two weeks after the pogrom, it established a Committee on Refugees, which undertook information campaigns aimed at persuading the public that refugees were loyal and hardworking. Unfortunately, the YWCA's national board soon lost interest in the project and declined to fund it. Jewish organizations ended up providing much of the committee's budget.

Christian Scientists, although small in number, had the opportunity to exercise influence through their mass-circulation newspaper, the *Christian Science Monitor*. But, true to their church's emphasis on the potential of prayer to heal all ills, the *Monitor's* editors argued that in response to Kristallnacht, "prayer...will do more than any amount of ordinary protests to heal the hate released in the last few days and to end injustices and excesses practiced in the name of anti-Semitism."

The *Monitor* did acknowledge that "finding havens for [the] refugees" was a necessity, but refrained from suggesting America as one of those havens.

Wanted: A Christian Answer
J. Parker Robinson
Christian Science Monitor
November 21, 1938
In this cartoon, Jews exiled from Germany march toward an uncertain fate, symbolized by the giant question mark. The cartoon's title, "Wanted: A Christian Answer," indicates the cartoonist's belief that Christians had a religious obligation to help.

Refugees Without Refuge
Jean Charlot
Commonweal, November 18, 1938
In this cartoon, which was published in the Catholic magazine *Commonweal,* Joseph, Mary, and baby Jesus are portrayed as Jewish refugees with no place to go.

Nazi Calvary
Vaughn Shoemaker
Chicago Daily News, November 17, 1938
Kristallnacht as a desecration of Christianity: the equivalent of Hitler turning Calvary, the site of the crucifixion, into an icon of Nazism.

Mark of the Beast
Henry Elderman
Washington Post, November 16, 1938
The cartoonist alludes to the reference in the New Testament to an evil or destructive creature bearing a distinguishing physical sign.

Since Thanksgiving Day followed soon after Kristallnacht, some cartoonists linked the two.

Mayflower
Cecil Jensen
Chicago Daily News, November 22, 1938
In the days following Kristallnacht, media reports indicated that the United States and other governments were devising plans to find havens for German Jews fleeing Hitler. These reports gave rise to hopes, as expressed in this cartoon, that "World Rescue Efforts" would soon save the stranded refugees. Unfortunately, however, those plans did not materialize.

There Isn't Any Turkey in Europe
Bruce Russell
Los Angeles Times
November 24, 1938

Although the term "luckless minorities" is vague, the proximity of the cartoon to the Kristallnacht pogrom and the bandages on the figure's face suggest that the reference is to Germany's Jews.

Pilgrims are Still Landing
Vaughn Shoemaker
Chicago Daily News
November 22, 1938

Plymouth Rock is a boulder on the Massachusetts shore which was traditionally identified as the spot where the pilgrims of the *Mayflower* first landed, in 1620. In this cartoon, Vaughn Shoemaker invokes those first pilgrims, who came to America in search of religious freedom. He links them to the "pilgrims who are still landing," that is, the refugees from Nazi Germany, who are standing atop a symbolic Plymouth Rock of their own which represents "Freedom of Worship."

23. NO ROOM FOR CHILDREN

In the spring of 1939, Congresswoman Edith Nourse Rogers (R-Massachusetts) and Senator Robert Wagner (D-New York) introduced legislation to permit 20,000 refugee children from Germany outside the quota system. The children would be 14 years old or younger, so there was no danger of them taking jobs away from American citizens. They would be cared for by private individuals and organizations, so they would not become a burden on the U.S. government.

Anne Frank

Many prominent Americans supported the Wagner-Rogers bill, including Catholic leaders such as His Eminence George Cardinal Mundelein; celebrities such as the famous actors Henry Fonda and Helen Hayes; and prominent political figures, including New York City Mayor Fiorello La Guardia, the governors of New York and Michigan, 1936 Republican presidential nominee Alf Landon, and his running mate, Frank Knox. Former First Lady Grace Coolidge announced that she and her neighbors in Northampton, Massachusetts, would take in twenty-five of the children.

More than eighty newspapers from thirty states endorsed the legislation. Although anti-immigration sentiment was known to be particularly strong in the South, twenty-six southern newspapers supported Wagner-Rogers.

Anti-foreigner groups, such as the Daughters of the American Revolution and the American Legion, lobbied vigorously against the bill. Some of them were motivated by dislike of foreigners in general, some by prejudice against Jews in particular. Mrs. Laura Delano Houghteling, who was President Franklin Roosevelt's cousin and the wife of the U.S. Commissioner of Immigration, articulated the sentiment of many opponents of the bill when she remarked at a dinner party that "20,000 charming children would all too soon grow up into 20,000 ugly adults."

During the public debate over the bill, and in the hearings that were held before Congress, opponents mustered every conceivable argument. Some went so far as to charge that the bill would harm Germany's Jews by breaking up their families. Other opponents claimed that since the legislation did not specify that the children had to be refugees, it was possible that 20,000 young Nazis would be brought to the United States. But the main argument was that Wagner-Rogers was a conspiracy to undermine the immigration system in order to eventually bring in a flood of immigrants.

President Franklin D. Roosevelt refused to take a position on the bill. When Congresswoman Caroline O'Day wrote to the White House to ask whether the president favored or opposed Wagner-Rogers, FDR returned the letter to his secretary with a note: "File No Action / FDR." Without presidential leadership, the legislation was doomed.

One of those who could have benefited from the bill was Anne Frank, the famous teenage Holocaust diarist.

At the time the Wagner-Rogers bill was being debated in Congress, the Franks were living in Holland, after fleeing from Nazi Germany. This was before the Holocaust began, and before Anne and her family went into hiding in an attic in German-occupied Amsterdam. The Franks hoped to immigrate to the United States. Anne's father, Otto Frank, filled out the small mountain of required application forms and obtained supporting affidavits from the family's relatives in Massachusetts. But that was not enough to satisfy the U.S. officials in charge of deciding who received permission and who was denied.

Even though the Franks as a family did not receive visas to the U.S., if the Wagner-Rogers bill had passed, Anne, who was then 10 years old, and her sister Margot, who was 13, could have qualified to come to America. Anne's mother, Edith, wrote to a friend in 1939: "I believe that all Germany's Jews are looking around the world, but can find nowhere to go."

One year later, however, there was a new campaign to bring children to America--British children. In response to the massive German bombing of London and other cities in 1940, the Roosevelt administration and Congress, with strong public support, quickly made changes to U.S. immigration law so that British children could be brought over without going through the usual bureaucratic procedures or requiring financial guarantees from individual American citizens. Several thousand British children were sheltered in the United States.

Most of those who opposed Wagner-Rogers did not object to bringing British children to the United States. These children were seen as ethnic kin--they were descended from the same people who were America's founding fathers. Unlike the German Jewish children, these kids were "just like us."

Adolf the Wolf
Dr. Seuss
PM
October 1, 1941

"America First" was an extremist movement in the late 1930s and early 1940s that believed problems such as Hitler's occupation of other countries and persecution of the Jews were none of America's business.

"...and the Wolf chewed up the children and spit out their bones... But those were Foreign Children and it really didn't matter."

126

24. ESCAPE TO FREEDOM

Throughout history, many totalitarian regimes have refused to permit scientists, artists, and other intellectuals to emigrate and instead forced them to work for the state. The Nazis, by contrast, undertook to drive out such individuals, despite the damage their departure would do to German society. Adolf Hitler reportedly said in 1933, "If the dismissal of Jewish scientists means the annihilation of contemporary German science, then we shall do without science for a few years."

Ostracizing, impoverishing, and encouraging the emigration of the intellectuals was a way for the Nazis to demonstrate their utter contempt for the cultural contributions of Jews and others whom they considered degenerates. Scientific achievements by Jews were regarded by Hitler as inherently tainted and therefore equally objectionable.

Many of the exiled German artists and scientists fled to neighboring France. In May 1940, the Nazis invaded and occupied France. By that time, Hitler was moving away from his previous policy of encouraging emigration, so the refugee intellectuals needed to be smuggled out of France.

Varian Fry in Vichy France, 1940.

SIX FAKE WIVES

Sponsored by a group called the Emergency Rescue Committee, a young American journalist, Varian Fry, traveled to France in late 1940 to organize their escape. Arriving with $3,000 taped to his leg to avoid detection by the authorities, Fry assembled a remarkable team of activists to carry out the operation. One was Charles Fawcett, a former professional wrestler from South Carolina. He took part in bogus marriages to six different women in one three-month period so that they would be released from French concentration camps and qualify for visas to the United States.

Also part of this effort were the Reverend Waitstill Sharp, a Unitarian minister from Massachusetts, and his wife Martha. In one instance, they rescued an anti-Nazi member of the Czech parliament by sneaking him out of a hospital morgue in a body bag. Hiram "Harry" Bingham IV, an American diplomat in France—and son of the famous explorer on whom the movie character of Indiana Jones was based—helped break the novelist Lion Feuchtwanger out of a detention camp by dressing him in women's clothes and having him pose as Bingham's mother-in-law.

World famous scientists, musicians, and painters left their belongings behind, donned field laborers' clothing, and marched with Fry to vineyards in the Pyrenees Mountains along the French-Spanish border, as if headed for a day of harvesting grapes. Once they reached Spain, they were able to continue on to Portugal, and from there they boarded ships bound for the United States. At the request of First Lady Eleanor Roosevelt, the president agreed to make a small number of visas available for exiled German intellectuals on the grounds that they represented the "cream of European civilization."

MISSION ABORTED

Fry's mission did not last long, however. The U.S. was not yet involved in World War II and the Roosevelt administration did not want to undermine its relations with Nazi Germany. When the Germans and their French partners complained about Fry's activities, the State Department canceled his passport, forcing him to leave France in 1941 and putting an end to his efforts. The Fry network rescued more than 2,000 refugees.

Many German Jewish refugees had a significant impact on American culture. Composer Franz Waxman, for example, who settled in Los Angeles in 1935, wrote the musical scores for a wide range of films, receiving 12 Academy Award nominations. He also founded the Los Angeles International Music Festival. Exiled theater director Max Reinhardt, who came to the U.S. in 1938, became a successful theater and film director, and established a school for acting in Los Angeles. The entire field of musicology in American universities is, to a large extent, the creation of German Jewish refugee music scholars.

AMERICA'S FAVORITE SURFER GIRL

Novelist Frederick Kohner, who arrived in 1933, was one of many German Jewish writers who found work as Hollywood screenwriters. He eventually hit it big with a series of novels about Gidget, a teenage surfer girl in Malibu, that led to a television series and several movies. A number of German Jewish refugee actors landed roles in anti-Nazi films, ironically sometimes playing Nazis since their accents were authentic.

Building designer Laszlo Moholy-Nagy, who moved to Chicago in 1937, established the School of Design, later part of the prestigious Illinois Institute of Technology, the first American school to offer a Ph.D. program in design. The influential graduate school of the New School for Social Research in New York City, was founded in 1933 for the purpose of providing an academic home for German Jewish refugee intellectuals. The new division was originally known as the University in Exile.

About 100 German Jewish physicists, including Albert Einstein and other Nobel Prize laureates, reached the United States in the 1930s and made significant contributions as university instructors and researchers. Einstein also played a crucial role in alerting President Franklin Roosevelt to Hitler's efforts to build an atomic bomb, and persuading him to initiate the development of America's own nuclear weapons.[19]

Germany's 'Gifts' to the Nations
Carl Rose
Jewish Daily Bulletin, April 30, 1933
A Nazi fist drives Jewish physicians, musicians, scientists, and novelists out of Germany. But, as the title of this cartoon suggests, the Germans were in effect giving "gifts" to other countries, because they benefited from the skills of the refugees whom they admitted.

Relativity
Edmund Duffy
Baltimore Sun, March 31, 1933

The famous German Jewish scientist Albert Einstein revolutionized modern physics and astronomy with his theory of relativity. Einstein was visiting the United States at the time of Hitler's rise to power in 1933, and chose to give up his German citizenship and remain in America, rather than return to live under Nazi rule. Einstein's decision was seen as a slap in the face to Hitler, and in this cartoon Einstein is shown snapping his fingers, to indicate that his action got Hitler's attention. But it soon became apparent that the Nazis in fact wanted to drive Jewish scientists out of the country, along with all other Jews, regardless of how much they would have contributed to Germany's scientific progress.

25. THE WHITE PAPER

In a 1917 policy statement known as the Balfour Declaration, the British government pledged to facilitate creation of a Jewish national home in Palestine, which had been the site of a Jewish state for more than 1,000 years in biblical times. In 1922, the League of Nations awarded England the mandate (the right to temporarily govern) for Palestine. It was expected that Jews would be free to immigrate to Palestine, purchase land, and take other nation-building steps. But in response to Palestinian Arab rioting in the 1930s, the British authorities began limiting Jewish immigration.

Dodging British patrols, immigration activists on the Palestine shore help Jewish refugees land, in 1939.

In May 1939, the British government adopted a new Palestine policy, known as the MacDonald White Paper, after Colonial Secretary Malcolm MacDonald. (Government policy papers were printed on white paper; laws and regulations were printed on blue paper.) The White Paper limited Jewish immigrants to a maximum of 75,000 over the next five years, after which immigration could continue only with the consent of Palestine's Arabs. The White Paper also restricted the right of Jews to purchase land from Arabs.

The new policy came at a time when the rise of antisemitism in Europe was forcing many Jews to emigrate, but no country in the West was willing to accept more than a few of them. At the very moment Palestine was most needed as a haven, Britain was shutting its gates. A leading British newspaper, the *Manchester Guardian*, called the White Paper "a death sentence on tens of thousands of Central European Jews."

President Roosevelt instructed Secretary of State Cordell Hull to privately inform the British that the United States did not approve of the new policy. But FDR was reluctant to clash with the British, so he said nothing about the White Paper in public and took no steps to pressure London to change its policy.

Jewish groups in the United States continued urging the British to open Palestine's doors, especially after the Nazis' mass murder of European Jews began in 1941. Palestine's close proximity to Europe made it a logical site to settle Jewish refugees. It was much easier for European Jews to reach Palestine by land or across the Mediterranean Sea, than to journey all the way across the Atlantic Ocean to North or South America. Nonetheless, the British refused to budge, convinced that permitting Jewish immigration would harm their relations with the Arab world.

Winston Churchill, as a member of the opposition in Parliament, denounced the White Paper as a "breach and repudiation" of England's promises to the Jewish people. However, when he became prime minister in 1940, Churchill kept the policy in force.

When the State of Israel was established in 1948, its first official act of government was to declare the White Paper "null and void."

Palestine Restricted
Arthur Szyk
New York Post, March 31, 1944
The White Paper was scheduled to expire on March 31, 1944, after which there would be no additional Jewish immigration without Arab approval. Szyk drew a vulture, with a swastika and skull-and-crossbones, swooping down on a group of Jewish refugees prevented from entering the padlocked door labeled "Palestine." The words in the upper right are from the biblical *Book of Job,* chapter 6, verse 27: "Yea, ye would cast lots upon the fatherless and dig a pit for your friend." Szyk included the verse as a criticism of the British for "digging a pit" for the Jews by shutting Palestine as the Nazis approach.

26. VOYAGE OF THE DOOMED

Refugees aboard the *St. Louis*.

In the aftermath of Kristallnacht, large numbers of Jews sought to flee Nazi Germany. A ship called the *St. Louis*, carrying 937 German Jewish refugees, set sail from Hamburg in May 1939. The passengers held visas to enter Cuba. But Cuban public opinion was turning sharply against immigration and, when the *St. Louis* docked at Havana, the Cuban government refused to honor the refugees' entry visas.

Some of the passengers' relatives had reached Cuba earlier and, as the *St. Louis* waited in the harbor, they boarded small boats that took them closer to the ship, to shout messages of encouragement and perhaps catch a glimpse of their loved ones.

Two young girls who had made the journey alone, seven year-old Renatta Aber and her five year-old sister, Evelyne, were brought to the front rail of the deck by a family friend so they could see their father, Dr. Max Aber, in one of the small boats below. But they had not seen him in a year and could not recognize him because of the distance. Ten year-old Marianne Bardeleben wore two Cuban hair clips that her father had sent to her in Germany and that her mother had kept secret from her until just that moment. She strained at the rail but could not pick her father out: there were just too many little boats in the harbor, too many desperate faces looking up at them.

Newlyweds Rosemarie and Otto Bergmann, however, had a pleasant surprise. As they looked out from the deck of the *St. Louis*, they could see that one of the men in the little boats was holding a white fox terrier aloft: it was their beloved dog, Oshey, whom they had sent ahead on a freighter with animal facilities.

THE SADDEST SHIP AFLOAT

When it became clear that Cuba would not admit the passengers, the *St. Louis*, which the *New York Times* called "the saddest ship afloat," sailed north to the coast of Florida. It hovered there for three days, hoping President Roosevelt would take pity on them and grant permission to land.

The passengers sent a telegram to the White House pleading for mercy and emphasizing that "more than 400 [of the refugees] are women and children." The reply came in the form of a Coast Guard cutter, which was

A LITTLE GIRL'S DISSENT

Eleven year-old Dee Nye, of Tacoma, Washington, wrote to First Lady Eleanor Roosevelt: "I am so sad the Jewish people have to suffer so. It hurts me so that I would give them my little bed if it was the last thing I had because I am an American. Let us Americans not send them back to that slaughter house. We have three rooms that we do not use. Mother would be glad to let someone have them."

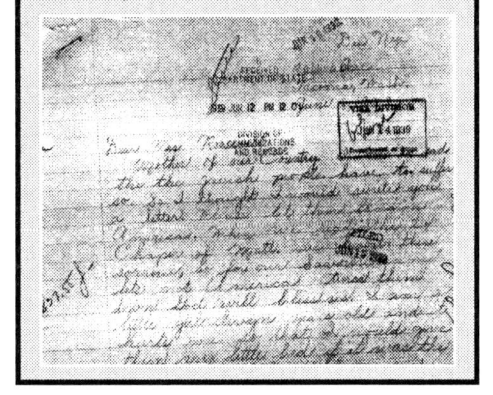

dispatched to the scene to make sure the *St. Louis* did not come closer to America's shore.

The United States had strict immigration laws that severely limited the number of foreigners who could be admitted. However, the president could have allowed the *St. Louis* passengers to stay temporarily, as tourists, in the Virgin Islands, a U.S. territory that was near Cuba. Or he could have issued an executive order to place the refugees in a temporary detention center in the United States until it was safe for them to return to Germany. But President Roosevelt feared such actions might be unpopular, so he chose to do nothing.

With America's doors closed, the *St. Louis* slowly sailed back towards Europe. A Nazi newspaper, *Der Weltkampf*, gloated: "We are saying openly that we do not want the Jews, while the democracies keep on claiming that they are willing to receive them—then leave them out in the cold."

Before the ship reached Europe, the governments of England, France, Belgium, and the Netherlands each agreed to accept a portion of the *St. Louis* passengers.

Those who were admitted to England survived the war. But less than a year later, the Germans invaded France, Belgium, and the Netherlands. Many of the *St. Louis* refugees who were admitted to those countries were eventually murdered in Nazi death camps.[20]

Another Refugee Ship
Jerry Doyle
New York Post, June 6, 1939
Although the hardships faced by unemployed college graduates hardly compared to the suffering of Germany's Jews under Hitler, this cartoon took advantage of the voyage of the *St. Louis* to make a point about a different issue.

Ashamed
Fred Packer
New York Daily Mirror, June 6, 1939
The Statue of Liberty was an obvious symbol for cartoonists commenting on the voyage of the *St. Louis*. The statue is often the first sight that new immigrants to the United States see as their ship approaches the port of New York City. A famous poem by Emma Lazarus, inscribed at the base of the statue, proclaims: "Give me your tired, your poor / Your huddled masses yearning to breathe free." The statue thus has come to symbolize the very concept of America as a haven for refugees from oppression. This cartoon appeared next to an editorial titled "Ashamed!," which noted that the statue in the cartoon was turning her head in shame at America's "Keep Out" policy. Although the *St. Louis* itself never actually sailed as far north as New York City, where the statue is located, Packer's depiction of the ship in front of the famous symbol of liberty offered a powerful commentary on President Roosevelt's stance.

The Wandering Jew
Edmund Duffy
Baltimore Sun, June 4, 1939
Like Eric Godal's "Wandering Jew" cartoon on page 95, Edmund Duffy here takes the medieval anti-Jewish myth of the wandering Jew and gives it a modern meaning. Here the Jewish refugees aboard the *St. Louis* have become, in effect, the real wandering Jews.

Tragedy at Sea
Herbert Block
NEA Syndicate, June 7, 1939
Mechanical failure resulted in two major submarine disasters shortly before this cartoon appeared. An American submarine, the *Squalus*, sank off the coast of New Hampshire on May 23, 1939, killing 26 of the 59 crewmen; the British submarine *Thetis* sank on June 1, 1939, drowning all 99 crew members. In this cartoon, Herbert Block contrasts these "failures of machinery," which were accidental, with the deliberate "failure of man" in the refusal of Cuba and the United States to admit the *St. Louis* refugees.

Rock of Ages, Cleft for Me
Jesse Cargill
King Features Syndicate, June 7, 1939
"Hatred and intolerance" divide the world and leave the "refugee ship" (the *St. Louis*) stranded on the high seas. The cartoon's title alludes to a famous 18th century Christian hymn about turning to God for protection.

27. WORLD WAR II BEGINS

On September 1, 1939, Germany invaded Poland. England and France responded by declaring war on Germany. World War II was underway. In the weeks following the invasion, the 3.3 million Jews of Poland, constituting the largest Jewish community in Europe, were frequently singled out for persecution by the German occupation forces.

German soldiers during the invasion of Poland.

Scattered reports reaching the United States during the fall of 1939 told of executions of groups of Polish Jewish civilians, Jews being consigned to slave labor, or other outrages. Sigrid Schultz, the *Chicago Tribune's* Berlin correspondent, later recalled how relatively easy it was to obtain information about Nazi atrocities in Poland:

"All one had to do was to go to one of the waiting rooms of the railroad stations in eastern Berlin and listen to [Nazi stormtroopers or military police] arriving from or leaving for the front. They seemed to enjoy describing how they had locked Poles and Jews into cellars and then thrown hand grenades through windows left open for the purpose."[21]

Part of the motivation for the invasion was Hitler's desire for what he called *Lebensraum*, or living space, for Germany. Even before the rise of the Nazis, some German nationalists had advocated *Lebensraum* as a way for Germany to acquire its neighbors' resources and improve its defenses. Hitler incorporated this idea into his racial and militarist philosophy of creating a vast empire over which Germans, as the "master race," would rule.

A "JEWISH RESERVATION" IN POLAND

Poland, Germany's neighbor to the east, was Hitler's first target. His intention was to strip Poland of its raw materials and to forcibly resettle large portions of the Polish population. This would make way for an influx of ethnic German families that had been living beyond Germany's borders. As part of this strategy, the Nazis initially decided to create a large "Jewish reservation" around the Polish city of Lublin, where German and Polish Jews would be concentrated.

In late 1939 and early 1940, about 95,000 Jews from Germany, Austria, and Czechoslovakia were deported to Lublin. Many died of starvation or disease during the deportation process or in Lublin, where some of the deportees were consigned to slave labor. By April 1940, however, Hitler dropped the plan to make Lublin into a Jewish region and began focusing instead on the idea of deporting all of Europe's Jews to the island of Madagascar, off the southeast coast of Africa. That plan, too, never materialized.

"Keep Moving!"
Vaughn Shoemaker
Chicago Daily News, September 1939

Outstretched Hand
Edmund Duffy
Baltimore Sun, October 7, 1939

Lebensraum for the Conquered
David Low
London Evening Standard, January 20, 1940
Hitler's demand for more *Lebensraum,* or living space, for Germans is contrasted with the "living hell" of the Lublin district, in Nazi-occupied Poland, to which Jews from all around Poland were deported by the Nazis in 1939-1940. Many died there from starvation, disease, and the rigors of slave labor.

28. THE HOLOCAUST BEGINS

The German mass murder of European Jewry proceeded in conjunction with Hitler's invasion of the Soviet Union in June 1941. Some of the largest Jewish communities in Europe were situated in the areas of Western Russia that lay directly in the path of the advancing German armies. The death camps, with their gas chambers and crematoria, were still under construction. The first mass killings were accomplished by mobile execution squads, known as *Einsatzgruppen*, that took hundreds, sometimes thousands, of Jews into nearby forests or ravines, compelled them to dig mass graves, and then machine-gunned them into the pits. Ultimately, between one and two million Jews were murdered in this fashion.

Jews executed in an East European forest, 1941.

Information about these massacres leaked out through a variety of sources, including escapees, foreign journalists, diplomats of neutral countries who learned of the murders through their contacts, and participants in the killings who returned home and boasted to friends. During the summer of 1941, fragmentary reports about the killings began appearing in the American press.

More detailed information soon arrived. On October 26, 1941, for example, the *New York Times* cited "letters reaching Hungary from Galicia" and "eye-witness accounts of Hungarian officers" returning from the front, which described between 10,000 and 15,000 Jews being "machine-gunned as they prayed in their synagogues" and elsewhere. "The deaths are reported to have been so numerous that bodies floated down the Dniester [river] with little attempt made to retrieve and bury them."

BABI YAR

Kiev, capital of the Soviet Union's Ukraine region, was home to 160,000 Jews on the eve of World War II. About 100,000 were able to flee before the Germans occupied the city in September 1941. All Jews were ordered to gather at an assembly point in the center of the city on September 28 from which, the Nazis said, they would be taken for "resettlement." The fact that the assembly site was adjacent to a railway station helped convince many that they were, indeed, simply being relocated. Tens of thousands reported to the designated location, among them a large number of children, the elderly, and the physically infirm: those for whom escape had been too difficult. They were then marched past the city limits to a ravine known as Babi Yar.

Ukrainian guards ordered the Jews to undress and savagely beat those who moved too slowly. The naked victims were then led, in groups of ten, to the edge of the ravine and then machine-gunned so they fell into the mass grave. At some points during the slaughter, the Jews were made to lie face down on top of the other corpses, and were shot at close range by individual German executioners.

Over the course of two days, 33,771 Jews were murdered in Babi Yar, according to German records. It was the single largest massacre of this kind to take place during the Holocaust. In the months to follow, other Jews who were captured in the area, as well as non-Jewish political prisoners and Soviet prisoners of war, were also killed there. According to Soviet researchers, an estimated 100,000 people were slaughtered in Babi Yar between 1941 and 1943.

AN ACTRESS ESCAPES

Dina Pronicheva, a young Jewish actress with the Kiev Puppet Theater, was among those who were lined up to be shot, but she jumped into the mass grave a split second before the gunfire and pretended to be dead. All around her she heard "strange submerged sounds, groaning, choking, and sobbing: many of the people were not dead yet." German soldiers jumped into the pit to shoot any survivors. One became suspicious of Dina. He kicked her in the chest and stepped on her hand, breaking it. But she remained limp and in the darkness he could not see that she was breathing.

Then came "a clatter of spades and then heavy thuds as the earth and sand landed on the bodies [but] the Ukrainian policemen up above were apparently tired after a hard day's work, too lazy to shovel the earth in properly, and once they had scattered a little in they dropped their shovels and went away." When they departed, Dina was able to pull herself out of the mass grave and escape. She was one of only three known survivors of Babi Yar.[22]

"MAMA! MAMA!"

Frida Michelson, a young seamstress, was among the Jews marched to the Rumbula forest, in German-occupied Latvia, on December 8, 1941. When they reached the spot where the women were forced to undress, she dove under the pile of clothing. "Some object hit me on the back, then another," she later recalled. "More objects were falling on me. Finally, I realized that these were shoes because they fell in pairs.... The load was heavy but I did not dare move a muscle....I could hear people crying bitterly, parting with each other....Finally the cries and moaning ceased, the shooting stopped. I could hear shovels working not far away. Probably to cover the bodies....A mountain of footwear was pressing down on me. My body was numb from cold and immobility....The snow under me melted from the heat of my body. I was lying in a puddle of water—cold water....Quiet for a while. Then, from the direction of the trench, a child's cry: 'Mama! Mama! Mamaaa!' A few shots. Quiet. Killed."[23]

Information about the Babi Yar massacre was slow to reach the free world. The initial reports were fragmentary and corroboration was hard to come by. Hence, the slaughter received little attention in the U.S. press, which helps explain why there were no editorial cartoons about it.

Babi Yar became the subject of controversy in postwar Russia. The Soviet regime, determined to stamp out symbols of Jewish national identity, refused to erect a monument to the victims of the massacre. The renowned poet Yevgeny Yevtushenko wrote a widely-circulated poem about Babi Yar in 1961, which the famous Soviet composer Dmitri Shostakovich set to music. This was followed, in 1966, by a powerful documentary novel, *Babi Yar*, by Anatoly Kuznetsov. As public interest and pressure grew, the Soviet authorities reluctantly set up a memorial at Babi Yar, but the plaque described the dead only as "victims of fascism," with no reference to Jews.

Enemies of the Third Reich
Arthur Szyk
American Hebrew
July 18, 1941

The Nazis justified their violence against Jews by claiming that the Jews were dangerous "enemies" of Germany, as in the title of this cartoon. Szyk's illustration highlights the absurdity of this accusation, showing that Hitler's Jewish victims, far from endangering Germany, were unarmed, destitute civilians, often children or the elderly.

Reproduced with the cooperation of The Arthur Szyk Society - Burlingame, CA - www.szyk.org

"Dear brothers in the Holy Land! For this Passover, you need to send only one box of matzohs…"

Letter from Exile
Yosef Bass
Ha'aretz
November 12, 1943

This cartoon appeared in the Hebrew-language newspaper *Ha'aretz*, in British-ruled Palestine. According to a news report reaching Palestine, only one Jew was left alive in the city of Kiev when the Soviets liberated it from the Germans in November 1943.

Berlin Sportpalast
Arthur Szyk
New York Post, October 2, 1942 & ***Newsweek,*** October 12, 1942
When the Berlin Sportpalast opened in 1910, it was the largest indoor meeting hall in the world, with a seating capacity of 14,000. Later, it became the site for many Nazi party rallies and speeches by Hitler. The word "Winterhilfe," in the lower left of Szyk's cartoon, alludes to a famous speech Hitler gave at the Sportpalast in 1940 in which he announced his plan for a massive air bombardment of England. This cartoon was drawn in response to a speech by Hitler at the Sportpalast on September 30, 1942, in which he vowed, "It will not be the Aryan nation which will be wiped out, but Jewry…[T]he Jews once laughed at my prophecies…but I can assure you that everywhere they will stop laughing. With these prophecies, I shall prove to be right!" The skull under Hitler's boot is labeled "Jude," the German word for "Jew."

29. THE "LIBERATION" THAT WASN'T

On November 8, 1942, American and British forces, under the command of U.S. General Dwight Eisenhower, invaded Nazi-occupied Morocco, Algeria, and Tunisia. It took the Allies just eight days to defeat the Germans and their Vichy (pro-Nazi) French partners in the region.

For the 330,000 Jews of North Africa, the Allied conquest was heaven-sent. The Vichy regime that had ruled since the summer of 1940 had stripped the region's Jews of their civil rights, severely restricted their entrance to schools and some professions, confiscated Jewish property, and tolerated sporadic pogroms against Jews by local Arabs. In addition, thousands of Jewish men were hauled away to forced-labor camps. Now, it seemed, all that was about to change. President Roosevelt, in his victory announcement, pledged "the abrogation of all laws and decrees inspired by Nazi governments or Nazi ideologists."

British troops advancing in North Africa, November 1942.

But there turned out to be a discrepancy between FDR's public rhetoric and his private feelings.

Among those taken prisoner on the first day of the battle was Admiral Francois Darlan, a senior leader of the Vichy French regime. In exchange for Darlan ordering his forces in Algiers to cease fire, President Roosevelt agreed to leave Darlan in charge of the newly-liberated North African territories. Many of FDR's supporters back home were appalled at the president's alliance with a prominent Nazi collaborator. "[It] sticks in the craw of majorities of the British and French, and of democrats everywhere, [that] we are employing a French Quisling as our deputy in the government of the first territory to be reoccupied," an editorial in *The New Republic* complained.

The Darlan government was in no rush to give equal rights to local Jews. Neither was President Roosevelt. On January 17, 1943, FDR met in Casablanca, Morocco, with Major-General Charles Nogues, one of the leaders of the new "non-Vichy" Darlan regime. When the conversation turned to the question of civil rights for North African Jews, Roosevelt said: "The number of Jews engaged in the practice of the professions (law, medicine, etc) should be definitely limited to the percentage that the Jewish population in North Africa bears to the whole of the North African population."

The transcript of the meeting continued: "The President stated that his plan would further eliminate the specific and understandable complaints which the Germans bore toward the Jews in Germany, namely, that while they represented a small part of the population, over fifty percent of the lawyers, doctors, school teachers, college professors, etc., in Germany, were Jews." (Those numbers were erroneous; only about 20% of German lawyers were Jewish, 11% of doctors, 9% of teachers, and 4% of college professors.)

THE SPIRIT OF THE SWASTIKA

The Allies permitted nearly all the original senior officials of the Vichy regime in North Africa to remain in the new government. The Vichy "Office of Jewish Affairs" continued to operate, as did the forced labor camps in which thousands of Jewish men were being held.

American Jewish leaders were reluctant to publicly take issue with the Roosevelt administration, but, by the spring of 1943, they began speaking out. The American Jewish Congress and the World Jewish Congress charged that "the anti-Jewish legacy of the Nazis remains intact in North Africa" and urged FDR to eliminate the Vichy laws. "The spirit of the Swastika hovers over the Stars and Stripes," Benzion Netanyahu, director of the U.S. wing of the Revisionist Zionists and father of a future Israeli prime minister, charged. Benzion Netanyahu, director of the U.S. wing of the Revisionist Zionists and father of a future Israeli prime minister. A group of Jewish GIs in Algiers protested directly to U.S. ambassador Robert Murphy. Editorials in a number of American newspapers echoed this criticism.

At first, Roosevelt administration officials dug in their heels. Undersecretary of State Sumner Welles insisted that, in theory, the region was no longer under Allied military occupation and the U.S. could not dictate how the local government ran things. Technically, Welles was correct but, in practice, America had significant influence over the Darlan government's policies. Eventually, after numerous public protests, the Roosevelt administration agreed to make it clear to the local authorities that the anti-Jewish measures needed to be repealed.

In April 1943, the Darlan government officially announced the shutdown of the camps, but some of them continued operating well into the summer. The Jewish quotas in school and professions were gradually phased out. In May, the racial laws in Tunisia were abolished, although it took several more months until the Allies finally released two hundred Italian Jews who were being held in a Tunisian forced labor camp because they were citizens of an Axis country. On October 20, nearly a year after the Allied liberation, full rights for North African Jews were at last reinstated.[24]

A PRISON WITHIN THE PRISON

If a prisoner in the forced labor camp of Djelfa, in Algeria, misbehaved, he would be placed in the camp's prison. A former inmate described conditions there: "Often up to three prisoners were piled up in a cell. No straw mattresses were given and it was forbidden to bring in more than one blanket....There was no lighting. There was no period for outdoor exercise. Food consisted of six ounces of bread per day and two measures of always meatless camp soup. In winter it was freezing and the more so as the panes of the windows beneath the ceiling were broken..."

Jews in Tunisia being taken away to a slave labor camp

"For a moment I thought it was my cousin!"

Internment Camp
Eric Godal
PM, February 3, 1943
Many Jewish soldiers serving in the United States Army had relatives among the Jews under Hitler's rule. This cartoon highlights that connection, to help illustrate the absurdity and injustice of North African Jews still being held in forced labor camps even though the Allies had already liberated the region from the pro-Nazi Vichy forces several months earlier.

Thru Darkest North Africa
Carl Rose
PM, April 15, 1943
This sarcastic "political travelogue" lambasted the Allies for allowing the pro-Nazi Vichyites to remain in power after the liberation of the region.

30. DR. SEUSS AND THE HOLOCAUST

French Jews being deported to Auschwitz, in 1942.

On July 16, 1942, 15 year-old Annie Kriegel was sitting in her Paris high school classroom, taking an exam, when her mother suddenly burst into the room and warned her not to come home—the Nazis were preparing to round up and deport any Jews they could get their hands on.

Annie found a place to stay that night. The next morning, as she later recalled, she was making her way towards the city's Jewish quarter when, "at the crossing of the rue de Turenne and the rue de Bretagne, I heard screams rising to the heavens." They were "not cries and squawks such as you hear in noisy and excited crowds, but screams like you used to hear in hospital delivery rooms. All the human pain that both life and death provide. A garage there was serving as a local assembly point, and they were separating the men and women." Stunned, the teenager sat down on a nearby park bench. "It was on that bench that I left my childhood."[25]

Over the course of the next two days, more than 13,000 Jews were rounded up in Paris by the Germans, with the active collaboration of the Vichy French government headed by Nazi supporter Pierre Laval. The majority of those arrested were couples with children. They were held for five excruciating days in the Velodrome d'Hiver stadium, in the summer heat without food or water. Eyewitnesses described it as "a scene from hell." Then, they were deported by train to the gas chambers of Auschwitz.

THE "SPORT" OF MASS MURDER

Theodor Geisel, who drew editorial cartoons for the New York City newspaper *PM* under the pen name "Dr. Seuss," addressed the news from France in his July 20, 1942 cartoon (see p.152). The future creator of such beloved classics as *The Cat in the Hat* and *Green Eggs and Ham* depicted a forest filled with Jewish corpses hanging from the trees. Adolf Hitler and the pro-Nazi French leader Pierre Laval were shown singing. Their first line, "Only God can make a tree," was taken from a famous poem by Joyce Kilmer about the unique beauty of trees. Their second line, "To furnish sport for you and me," was concocted by Hitler and Laval to celebrate their "sport" of mass murder.

> **YERTLE THE TURTLE AND THE NAZIS**
>
> At first glance, the title story of Dr. Seuss's 1958 best-seller, *Yertle the Turtle and Other Stories*, seems to be an ordinary child's fable. But in fact Seuss created a thinly-veiled attack on totalitarianism, using images of a tower of turtles that originally came from one of his 1940s political cartoons. Yertle is the king of a turtle pond who exploits his fellow-turtles in order to increase his power and personal glory. Furious when he realizes the moon is higher than he is, Yertle commands his subjects to form themselves into a tower so that he can stand on top of them and reach the sky. Seuss said later that Yertle was meant to symbolize Hitler.

Dr. Seuss
PM, July 20, 1942

Joyce Kilmer, the writer whose famous poem, "Trees," is the basis for this cartoon, had a particular connection to France: while serving in the U.S. army in World War I, he was killed in a battle there. He was posthumously awarded the Croix de Guerre (War Cross) by the French government, and is buried in a military cemetery in France. This may explain, in part, why Dr. Seuss chose to link him to this cartoon about the fate of French Jewry. Seuss may also have felt a kinship to Kilmer as a fellow-poet.

31. GENOCIDE CONFIRMED

In late 1941 and early 1942, the Germans began deporting Jews to camps in occupied Poland, where they were systematically put to death with poison gas. Information about these death camps did not immediately reach the outside world. Hence, well into 1942, most Allied officials and American Jewish leaders assumed that the killings were random wartime atrocities rather than part of an organized Nazi strategy.

Polish Jewish children being rounded up for deportation from the Lodz Ghetto, September 1942.

These assumptions began to change with the arrival of two new reports from Europe in the summer of 1942. A report smuggled from Poland in June 1942 disclosed that the Germans had "embarked on the physical extermination of the Jewish population on Polish soil," and had already murdered an estimated 700,000 Polish Jews. It even described a mobile death van that the Nazis had designed in the Chelmno camp, in which the exhaust fumes were pumped back into the vehicle, and that was used before the gas chamber technique was perfected.

In August 1942, rescue activists in Switzerland learned from a senior German source about Hitler's annihilation plan. In a telegram to Jewish leaders in the United States and England, they reported: "In Fuhrer's headquarters plan discussed and under consideration according to which all Jews in countries occupied or controlled Germany numbering 3 1/2 - 4 millions should after deportation and concentration in East be exterminated at one blow...the action reported planned for autumn methods under discussion including prussic acid."

"COLD-BLOODED EXTERMINATION"

When Jewish leaders approached the State Department with this information, they were told it could not be confirmed and the Jews were likely being deported to forced labor camps. But after further investigation, the State Department confirmed, in November, that the telegram was accurate, and Jewish leaders in the United States publicized the news.

In early December, British Jewish leaders and Members of Parliament began pressing the British government to respond to the mass murder. In an attempt to deflect the growing criticism, British officials proposed to the Roosevelt administration that the Allies issue a statement condemning the killings.

London's first draft referred to "reports from Europe which leave no room for doubt" that systematic annihilation was underway. The State Department objected to that phrase on the grounds that—as one U.S. official complained—it could "expose [the Allies] to increased pressure from all sides to do something more specific in order to aid these people." The final statement, released on December 17, omitted the phrase "which leave no room for doubt."

The declaration condemned the Nazis' "bestial policy of cold-blooded extermination" and warned that the perpetrators would face postwar punishment. This represented the first time the Allies officially acknowledged the genocide, although that word was not yet in vogue. The statement was signed by the United States, Great Britain, the Soviet Union, and the governments-in-exile of eight German-occupied countries. Pope Pius XII declined to sign because, the papal secretary explained, the Vatican preferred to condemn war crimes in general rather than single out any specific atrocities.

The declaration contained no reference to the Allies taking any steps to rescue Jews. As one senior State Department official remarked to his colleagues during the discussion over the wording, "The plight of the unhappy peoples of Europe, including the Jews, can be alleviated only by winning the war." This sentiment reflected the Roosevelt administration policy that would come to be known as "rescue through victory."[26]

News From Abroad
Stan Fraydas
PM, January 20, 1943
Nazi propagandists routinely claimed that Allied military attacks on Germany were the result of an international Jewish conspiracy, and some anti-Jewish actions that the Nazis undertook were described by Hitler as "punishment" for Allied raids. In December 1942, the Allies confirmed that the Germans were in the process of massacring millions of European Jews. Just a few weeks later, on January 16, 1943, British planes carried out the first major bombing of Berlin in more than a year. Thus, in this cartoon, senior Nazi official Heinrich Himmler asks Hitler whom they can blame for the bombing of Berlin if all the Jews are dead.

32. THE GAS CHAMBERS

It is sometimes assumed that it was only after the end of World War II that the international community learned details of the Holocaust, such as the Germans' use of poison gas for mass murder. In fact, as the cartoons in this chapter demonstrate, the role of gas chambers was so widely known at the time that even some cartoonists made reference to them.

The Germans first began employing poison gas to murder civilians in 1940, as part of their program to eliminate German citizens who were mentally or physically handicapped. This was part and parcel of the Nazi racial ideology of weeding out individuals who were deemed "inferior." These killings were kept secret in order to avoid protests by the German public. Disabled men and women were taken from state institutions that were supposedly caring for them, and brought to gas chambers disguised as shower rooms, where they were asphyxiated. This "racial hygiene" program was known as "T4," after the address of the government office responsible for it. An estimated 200,000 people were murdered in this fashion.

Jewish women prisoners at Auschwitz had their heads shaved shortly before they were taken to the gas chambers.

A GAS CHAMBER ON WHEELS

The Germans later applied their experience and technology from the T4 campaign, and many of its personnel, to their war against the Jews. The first mass killings of Jews by the Nazis, in occupied Russia in 1941, were carried out through machine-gun massacres. At the same time, German officials seeking a more efficient method of execution were developing a mobile gas van. About 50 people could be fit in the vehicle at a time. The exhaust system was rewired so that it pumped its carbon monoxide fumes back into the van. These vehicles were first used on a regular basis in the Chelmno camp, in German-occupied Poland, in late 1941.

Stationary gas chambers began operating in the Belzec camp in February 1942. Later that spring, they were inaugurated in Sobibor, Treblinka, and Auschwitz. Typically the victims were told they were being taken for delousing. Orchestras composed of inmates were sometimes used to lull the victims into a false sense of security as they were led to their deaths. The gas chambers were disguised as shower rooms, complete with shower heads from which the gas was emitted.

To enhance the ruse, the rooms were stocked with fake soap bars made of stone. At Treblinka, the gas chamber buildings were surrounded by flower beds. After the victims undressed, their hair was cut off to be used for stuffing German pillows and mattresses. The deception process was effective. Thomas "Toivi" Blatt, a prisoner who was assigned to cut off the victims' hair, later recalled how one Dutch Jewish woman asked him not to cut her hair too short: "She still believed she was not going to die."

The prisoners were then ordered to enter the "shower" area, sometimes with their arms raised so that the largest possible number of people could be crammed in. The gassing took

20 to 30 minutes. Auschwitz commander Rudolf Höss later said that he did not know of a single instance in which someone survived a gassing.

There were, however, a number of instances in which the gas chambers malfunctioned while filled with prisoners, thus temporarily sparing their lives. It also happened on various occasions that individuals were pulled out of the gas chambers at the last moment, usually because they were needed for labor. When a round of gassings was completed, the bodies of the dead were taken to nearby crematoria and incinerated.

SELECTING THE VICTIMS

Sam Bankhalter, survivor of Auschwitz: "Whole families came into Auschwitz together, and you got to Dr. [Josef] Mengele, who was saying, 'Right, left. Left, right,' and you knew, right there, who is going to the gas chamber and who is not. Most of the men broke down when they knew their wives and their kids—three, five, nine year-olds—went into the gas chambers. In fact, one of my brothers committed suicide in Auschwitz because he couldn't live with knowing his wife and children were dead. I was able to see my family when they came into Auschwitz in 1944. I had a sister; she had a little boy a year old. Everybody that carried a child went automatically to the gas chamber, so my mother took the child. My sister survived, but she still suffers, feels she was a part of killing my mother."[27]

Inside one of the gas chambers at Auschwitz

THE TRUTH REVEALED

The first substantial report about the Nazis' use of gas against Jewish prisoners reached the West in May 1942. Known as the Bund Report (because it originated with the Jewish Socialist Bund underground in Poland), it revealed that an average of 1,000 Jews had been killed in Chelmno each day "by gassing," in "special automobiles" designed for murder. A prominent article in the *London Daily Telegraph* on June 25, headlined "Germans Murder 700,000 Jews in Poland," included the subtitle, "Travelling Gas Chambers."

Additional information about gassings continued to arrive in the months to follow. By November, the *New York Times* was reporting that "concrete buildings on the former Russian frontiers are used by the Germans as gas chambers in which thousands of Jews have been put to death." References to gas chambers appeared in many subsequent newspaper reports about the Nazi persecution of European Jewry.

How the Beastly Business Begins
David Low
London Evening Standard, June 18, 1943
One of the very few cartoons to explicitly show Jews being taken to be gassed.

"Let's not kill fascism—let's hold an exhibition."

International Exhibition
Eric Godal
PM, April 13, 1944
Godal addressed the issue of gas chambers in a somewhat roundabout way. The previous day, *PM* had reported that the Roosevelt administration intended to participate in an international trade fair hosted by the fascist Franco government of Spain and including exhibits by Axis regimes. Godal included a gas chamber in his satirical version of what the German exhibit might contain.

33. TRAINS OF DEATH

The main killing centers were set up in German-occupied Poland. Jews from throughout Europe were brought there by rail in train cars that were ordinarily used for transporting cattle. So many people were forced into each car that there was no room for anyone to sit down. No food was given to the prisoners, and no sanitary facilities were provided other than a bucket. The trip usually took several days, longer if the train had to wait at a junction for its turn, while other trains passed first. Many of the deportees died en route.

Jews being forced into the cattle cars of trains that would transport them to the Auschwitz death camp.

"It was hell in the [cattle car]," 13 year-old Maria Ezner later recalled, of her deportation from Hungary. "It was dark, in the day too. At night it was like in a sack...We were hungry, we didn't eat....People shouted at each other. People went mad and pulled out their hair, and screamed. There were old people, ill people....A little air came in at the windows, and there was a fight for a spot near there. 'Let me get to the window! I can't get any air!' Hysterical cries are in my memory....On the third day, early in the morning, we came to the camp. We saw barbed-wire fences and gates, and German soldiers with great German shepherd dogs. We saw women holding whips....They were Ukrainians. [They] came with their whips and beat us out of the wagons."

A JUMP FROM A SPEEDING TRAIN

Despite the fact that armed German guards were posted on the trains, a small number of deportees attempted to escape. Seventeen year-old Claire Probizor Schiffer, her husband, Phillip, and her father, Yehezkel, were deported from Belgium in April 1943. Claire had smuggled a saw onto the train and they planned to cut through the window bars and jump out. Then her father fell ill. "My father was unconscious and burning with fever," she later wrote. "I had to face up to the truth. He was not going to jump! I called Phillip over and told him, 'I won't jump from the train. I can't abandon my father.'"

Time was running out; Phillip insisted they jump before the train crossed the Belgian-German border, fearing it would be impossible afterwards. Although wracked with guilt, Claire was finally persuaded by her husband that if they did not escape, they would soon be murdered by the Nazis along with all the others in the car. As the train sped along at 50 mph, Claire and Philip sawed through the bars and jumped, tumbling down a steep embankment and, miraculously, emerging unharmed.[28]

The Nazi leadership placed such a high priority on killing Jews that until the final days of the war, trains that could have been used for transporting soldiers or military equipment were instead set aside to bring more Jews to the death camps. Some German Army officers protested that the policy was undermining the war effort, but to no avail.

In 1944, as Allied forces were advancing across Europe, Jewish organizations in the United States pleaded with the Roosevelt administration to bomb the railroad tracks leading to Auschwitz in order to disrupt the deportations, or bomb the gas chambers and

A MEETING IN TEL AVIV

A postscript from Claire Schiffer's memoir: "In June 1962, a little while after arriving in Israel, I was strolling down Dizengoff Street in Tel Aviv one night, when a woman grabbed my shoulder. 'Don't you recognize me?' she asked. 'I have been looking for you for 20 years. I have a message for you from your father.'" Claire was overcome with emotion: "All of the guilt feelings that had been bothering me for so long returned and grew stronger." The woman had been on the train car, next to her father, after they jumped. "And this is what she told me: 'A few hours before we arrived at [Auschwitz], your father opened his eyes....He called out your name and I told him, 'Your daughter jumped from the train on Belgian soil, with her husband.' After a few minutes, your father said to me: 'Listen, I want you to look for my daughter in every corner of the world, and tell her that I am very happy that she jumped from the train.' Soon afterwards, he passed away."

crematoria themselves. U.S. officials rejected the requests, claiming the only way for American planes to reach Auschwitz would be to divert them from battle zones elsewhere in Europe, where they were urgently needed. In truth, however, U.S. planes were already flying over Auschwitz, because they were bombing German oil factories located next to the camp.

Ironically, the Allies did bomb a number of railway junctions in Hungary in the summer of 1944 as part of their military strategy, at about the same time that the Nazis were deporting Jews from Hungary to Auschwitz. The Hungarian government, which initially cooperated with the Germans in the deportations, ended its cooperation in part because it mistakenly believed that the Allied bombings were in response to Jewish requests and would increase if the deportations continued. In at least once instance, an Allied bombing raid on Hungarian railway lines—near the northwestern city of Gyor—halted a train of deportees bound for Auschwitz, enabling some of them to escape.

Reproduced with the cooperation of The Arthur Szyk Society - Burlingame, CA - www.szyk.org

Who Cares?
Arthur Szyk
New York Post
June 1, 1943

*On he goes, though infinite the night,
And ghouls of blackness mercilessly stalking.*

Ghouls of Blackness
Arthur Szyk
The Answer, November 1944
Hitler and other Nazi leaders hover over gravestones with the names of the death camps "Oswiecim" (Auschwitz), "Tremblinka" (Treblinka), "Majdanek," and "Bel" (probably Belzec), as well as "Bialystok," a Polish town where thousands of Jews were massacred and additional tens of thousands of Jews were deported to the camps.

"I've settled the fate of Jews"—"And of Germans."

Jews to the Slaughter House
David Low
London Evening Standard, December 14, 1942
Low was one of the few cartoonists to refer to the Germans' use of cattle cars to transport Jews to their deaths.

34. BERMUDA: THE MOCK REFUGEE CONFERENCE

In early 1943, some British Members of Parliament and church leaders began calling for Allied action to rescue Jews from Hitler. In the United States, too, some prominent journalists and members of Congress urged prompt U.S. intervention on behalf of European Jews.

To head off this growing pressure, British officials suggested to the Roosevelt administration that the two governments should hold a conference on the refugee problem.

The British bluntly told their American counterparts their chief concern was that the Nazis might try to "embarrass" the Allies "by flooding them with alien immigrants." As a result, the main purpose of the conference would be to create the impression of Allied sympathy for the refugees without agreeing to any concrete plans to aid them.

American and British delegates at the Bermuda conference.

AWKWARD QUESTIONS

The U.S. accepted the British proposal and publicly suggested the conference be held in Ottawa, Canada. The Canadian government, however, had not been consulted and strongly objected to hosting the gathering. The Canadians were unwilling to take in Jewish refugees and feared that holding the conference in Ottawa would—as one official put it—lead to "awkward questions in Parliament and publicity in the press" about Canada's harsh refugee policy. The British proposed holding it in Washington; the U.S. suggested London. Both governments objected for the same reason as the Canadians. Finally they agreed on the island of Bermuda, far from the prying eyes of protesters and journalists, as the site for the conference.

Jewish organizations hoped to send a delegation to the Bermuda conference to propose specific methods of rescue, but the U.S. and British governments rejected that request. A group of Jewish members of Congress who met with President Roosevelt on April 1 also raised the idea of a Jewish delegation attending the conference. FDR turned them down.

WHAT TO DO WITH SO MANY JEWS?

The Bermuda conference opened on April 19. That same day, 4,000 miles away, German Army units commanded by General Juergen Stroop stormed into the Warsaw Ghetto to annihilate the ghetto and deport its remaining 50,000 Jewish residents to death camps.

The American and British delegates in Bermuda conferred for 12 days. The talks consisted largely of discussions about why various possibilities for rescue seemed unrealistic or politically undesirable. Although the proceedings were kept secret, it was clear from leaks to the press that there was little hope the Allies would develop serious rescue plans. One delegate

A SUICIDE IN LONDON

Despondent over the mass deportation of Warsaw's Jews-- including his own wife and son-- and the failure of the Bermuda conference, exiled Polish Jewish leader Szmul Zygielbojm took his own life in London on May 12, 1943. His suicide note declared: "The responsibility for the crime of the murder of the whole Jewish nationality in Poland rests first of all on those who are carrying it out, but indirectly it falls also upon the whole of humanity, on the peoples of the Allied nations and on their governments, who up to this day have not taken any real steps to halt this crime."

Szmul Zygielbojm

was quoted as telling reporters, "Suppose he [Hitler] did let 2,000,000 or so Jews out of Europe, what would we do with them?"

The *New York Times* reported, in the middle of the conference, that the delegates had decided "that the refugees should be kept as near as possible to the areas where they now are," because "from there they could most readily return to their own countries after the war." Keeping the Jews away, not rescuing them, was the priority at Bermuda.

The Bermuda meeting concluded on May 2, with no announcement of any significant Allied plans for rescue. Jewish leaders called the conference a "cruel mockery" and a "woeful failure."[31]

Non Stop Express to Bermuda
Yosef Bass
Ha'aretz, April 8, 1943
In this rare depiction of Roosevelt and Churchill, the two leaders are driving a bus to the Bermuda refugee conference. They refuse to pick up any of the Jewish leaders waiting on the curb; Jewish groups were denied access to the conference.

35. A DRAMATIC RESCUE FROM DENMARK

The Nazis invaded Denmark in 1940, but the Danes put up little resistance and the Germans agreed to let the Danish government continue functioning with greater autonomy than in other occupied countries. They also postponed taking steps against Denmark's 8,000 Jewish citizens. In the late summer of 1943, amid rising tensions between the occupation authorities and the Danish government, the Nazis declared martial law and decided the time had come to deport Danish Jews to the death camps.

Word of the Germans' intentions leaked out, sparking a spontaneous nationwide grassroots effort to help the Jews. Many Christian families hid Jews in their homes or farms and then smuggled them to the seashore late at night. From there, Danish fishermen took them across the Kattegat Straits to neighboring Sweden. This remarkable three-week rescue operation had the strong support of Danish church leaders, who used their pulpits to urge aid to the Jews, as well as of Danish universities, which shut down so that students could assist the smugglers. More than 7,000 Danish Jews reached Sweden and were sheltered there until the end of the war.

Danish Jews aboard a fisherman's boat, fleeing to the safety of Sweden.

A MIDNIGHT ESCAPE

Esther Finkler, a young newlywed, was hidden in a greenhouse, together with her husband and their mothers, "At night, we saw the [German] searchlights sweeping back and forth throughout the neighborhood," as the Nazis hunted for Jews.

One evening, a member of the Danish Underground arrived and drove the four "through streets saturated with Nazi stormtroopers," to a point near the shore. There they hid in an underground shelter, then in the attic of a bakery, until finally they were brought to a beach, where they boarded a small fishing vessel together with other Jewish refugees. "There were nine of us, lying down on the deck or the floor," Esther later recalled. "The captain covered us with fishing nets. When everyone had been properly concealed, the fishermen started the boat, and as the motor started to run, so did my pent up tears."

Then, suddenly, trouble. "The captain began to sing and whistle nonchalantly, which puzzled us. Soon we heard him shouting in German toward a passing Nazi patrol boat: '*Wollen sie einen beer haben?*' (Would you like a beer?)—a clever gimmick designed to avoid the Germans' suspicions." The ruse worked; the Germans went on their way.

"After three tense hours at sea," Esther recalled, "we heard shouts: 'Get up! Get up! And welcome to Sweden!' It was hard to believe, but we were now safe. We cried and the Swedes cried with us as they escorted us ashore. The nightmare was over."[32]

IT CAN BE DONE

The implications of the Danish rescue operation reverberated strongly in the United States. The Roosevelt administration had long insisted that the rescue of Jews from the Nazis was not possible. Refugee advocates such as the Bergson Group (also known as the Emergency Committee to Save the Jewish People of Europe) now cited the escape of Denmark's Jews as evidence that if the Allies were sufficiently interested, ways could be found to save many European Jews. The group sponsored a series of full-page advertisements in American newspapers about the Danish-Swedish effort, headlined "It Can Be Done!"

Thousands of New Yorkers jammed Carnegie Hall on October 31 for the Bergson Group's "Salute to Sweden and Denmark" rally. Keynote speakers included leading political and diplomatic officials, as well as one of the most prominent figures in Hollywood: Orson Welles, director and star of *Citizen Kane* and radio's *The War of the Worlds*. The Bergson Group's ability to attract a range of political and cultural celebrities impressed public opinion and strengthened its demands for U.S. intervention to aid the Jews.

Rescuers
Arie Navon
Davar, October 13, 1943
American cartoonists were reluctant to lampoon President Roosevelt, but cartoonists in the Palestine Jewish community were more forthright. This cartoon in the Hebrew-language daily *Davar* depicted Roosevelt and Churchill as lifeguards, with a life preserver labeled "Bermuda" (referring to the Bermuda refugee conference—see Chapter 34) at their feet. While the British and American leaders stand idly by, a scrawny man with a life preserver labeled "Sweden" dives into the swastika-infested waters. The title of the cartoon is a Hebrew word which means both "Lifeguards" and "Rescuers."

36. FIGHTING BACK

Throughout Nazi-occupied Europe, small groups of Jews undertook armed resistance against their oppressors, using weapons such as homemade bombs and guns stolen from German soldiers or purchased on the black market.

Thousands of Jews escaped into the forests of German-occupied Eastern Europe and joined up with groups of partisans, who engaged in guerrilla attacks against Nazi targets. In some instances, however, partisans were themselves antisemitic and turned against their Jewish comrades.

In more than 100 ghettos, Jewish rebels carried out acts of armed resistance. Although they knew their efforts could not succeed, fighting back boosted Jewish morale and diverted German military resources. Jewish prisoners in a number of death camps also staged revolts. In the Treblinka camp in August 1943 and in Sobibor two months later, prisoners stole weapons, attacked guards and, in a few cases, succeeded in escaping.

In Auschwitz, an armed revolt was organized in late 1944 by members of the Sonderkommando, Jewish prisoners whose lives were temporarily spared because they were needed for tasks such as removing the dead bodies from the gas chambers and maintaining the crematoria in which corpses were incinerated. Taking advantage of their access to the mass-murder machinery, and using gunpowder smuggled from a munitions factory in another part of the Auschwitz complex, the Sonderkommando succeeded in blowing up one of the crematoria before they were killed by the Germans.

The most sustained and best known of the revolts took place in the Warsaw Ghetto. After more than 250,000 Jews were deported from the ghetto to death camps in 1942-1943, and with the Germans preparing to deport the remaining 50,000, Jewish fighters staged a well-organized rebellion in April 1943. It took fully a month before the Nazis were able to fully suppress the revolt, which they accomplished by systematically burning down every building in the ghetto. For many months afterwards, pockets of fighters held out in underground bunkers.

While the revolt was underway, fragmentary news about the fighting was transmitted to Polish anti-Nazi activists outside the ghetto, and then broadcast to the West, where some of it appeared in major newspapers such as the *New York Times*. The Roosevelt administration did not consider sending any kind of aid to the rebels. In April 1944, President Roosevelt sent a message of greeting to a rally in New York City commemorating the revolt, in which he praised the fighters but did not mention that they were Jews. In August 1944, members of a Polish armed force, the Polish Home Army, staged a revolt of their own in Warsaw. American and

HEROINE OF THE REVOLT

Rosa Robota, a 23 year-old Polish Jewish refugee, was a key figure in the revolt at Auschwitz. She organized more than 20 of her coworkers in the munitions factory to hide bits of gunpower in special pockets that they sewed inside their dresses, which could be emptied to the ground by pulling a hidden string if they were in danger of being discovered. The slave laborers were often searched by German guards on their way to or from the munitions plant.

Rosa Robota

After the revolt was suppressed, the Nazis identified Rosa and three of her comrades. They were brutally tortured to death, but never surrendered the names of the others involved in the plot.[33]

British planes were sent to drop weapons and supplies to them, even though Allied officials expected that the majority of the materials would be intercepted by the Germans. The American and British governments regarded the Poles as important allies in World War II, but did not see Europe's Jews the same way.

Warsaw Jews
Fred Ellis
Daily Worker, August 19, 1944

The Repulsed Attack
Arthur Szyk
Morgen Zhurnal, April 7, 1944

We Will Never Go Back to the Ghetto
Arthur Szyk
The Answer, April 1945
A Warsaw Ghetto fighter mockingly holds up the order signed by Gestapo chief Heinrich Himmler to destroy the ghetto.

37. FDR AND THE HOLOCAUST

President Franklin D. Roosevelt.

Franklin D. Roosevelt was president throughout the entire Holocaust period, 1941-1945, and information about the mass killings was confirmed by late 1942. Nevertheless, he almost never mentioned the subject in public.

One of the rare occasions on which FDR did mention the plight of Europe's Jews was at a press conference in October 1943, when a reporter asked whether his administration was contemplating helping "Jewish victims of atrocities or persecution." President Roosevelt replied: "I don't know...that whole problem is—the heart's all right—it's a question of ways and means." In other words, he was claiming that in his heart, he wanted to help the Jews, but the "ways and means" could not be found.

"RESCUE THROUGH VICTORY"

Jewish organizations and other refugee advocates repeatedly approached the White House and State Department with specific proposals to aid the Jews. U.S. officials replied that rescue was possible only through military victory over the Nazis. The administration insisted, for example, that no ships were available to transport refugees from Europe to the Western hemisphere. Actually, however, American ships bringing supplies to U.S. troops returned empty to the United States and had to be weighed down with ballast, such as chunks of concrete, so they would not capsize.

Roosevelt administration officials also claimed that if the U.S. admitted more refugees, they would take jobs away from American citizens. Ironically, however, the Department of Agriculture in 1944 alone spent $30-million to import large numbers of Latin American workers, because there was a labor shortage caused by so many young men serving in the military.

The real reason for the administration's reluctance to assist Europe's Jews was that President Roosevelt did not want to have to bring large numbers of rescued refugees to America. At the same time, the British did not want to bring Jewish refugees to British-ruled Palestine, because of Arab opposition.

THE "DANGER" OF SAVING LIVES

FDR delegated management of the European Jewish question to the State Department. Officials there understood that taking affirmative steps to aid the Jews would create pressure for more immigration to the United States. Thus Cavendish W. Cannon, the assistant chief of the State Department's Division of European Affairs, candidly told a colleague in 1941 that he opposed rescuing 300,000 Jews from Rumania because it was "likely to bring about new pressure for an asylum in the western hemisphere."

Similarly, in May 1943, a senior official of the State Department's Visa Division, Robert Alexander, opposed rescue because it would "take the burden and the curse off Hitler." Likewise, R. Borden Reams of the State Department's Division of European Affairs wrote to colleagues in October 1943 of what he called "the danger that the German Government might agree to turn over to the United States and to Great Britain a large number of Jewish refugees."

At a meeting in the White House in 1943, British Foreign Minister Anthony Eden explained to President Roosevelt and Secretary of State Cordell Hull why he opposed Allied action to help the Jews of Bulgaria: "If we do that, then the Jews of the world will be wanting us to make similar offers in Poland and Germany." Roosevelt and Hull did not disagree with Eden's position.

Assistant Secretary of State Breckinridge Long.

No American cartoonist is known to have directly criticized President Roosevelt for his policies concerning Jewish refugees. This may have stemmed from a fear that challenging the president in the midst of the war might seem to be unpatriotic. Several cartoonists in British-ruled Palestine, however, were more forthright in their criticism of FDR and his administration, as the cartoons in this chapter demonstrate.

POSTPONE AND POSTPONE AND POSTPONE

The State Department official who was most directly responsible for administering policies affecting European Jewish refugees during the Holocaust was Breckinridge Long. The son of wealthy southern aristocrats, Long was a personal friend of Franklin Roosevelt before he was president, and became a major contributor to his political campaigns. In 1940, FDR appointed Long to be assistant secretary of state in charge of the State Department's "Special War Problems Division." That included the handling of visa applications from would-be immigrants.

Long was a vehement opponent of immigration. "We can delay and effectively stop for a temporary period of indefinite length the number of immigrants into the United States," he wrote in a memo to State Department colleagues in 1940. "We could do this by simply advising our consuls to put every obstacle in the way and to require additional evidence and to resort to various administration devices which would postpone and postpone and postpone the granting of the visas."

Congressman Emanuel Celler publicly charged that the State Department's methods for screening potential immigrants were "cold and cruel" and "glacier-like." Indeed, over 90% of the immigration quota places for citizens of Germany and Axis-occupied countries sat unused between 1941 and 1945. More than 190,000 people could have been saved with those quota places.

ACQUIESCENCE

Long and his State Department colleagues also sought to suppress Holocaust-related information that reached the United States. They were concerned that publicity about the atrocities would put pressure on the Roosevelt administration to help the Jews. But their suppression of the news inadvertently triggered a crisis that would lead to the exposure of their actions.

These events began in the spring of 1943, when American Jewish organizations applied for government permission to send funds to Europe to help shelter and rescue refugees. Their application was sent first to Josiah E. DuBois, Jr., an official of the Treasury Department, who approved it. But it also required the endorsement of the State Department, which was not forthcoming.

Suspicious about the delays, DuBois asked a friend inside the State Department to let him see its private files on the refugee issue. In those files, DuBois discovered that senior State Department officials had been obstructing opportunities to rescue Jews and blocking the transmission of news about the mass killings.

In an attempt to throw DuBois off his trail, Long altered a telegram that Treasury Secretary Henry Morgenthau, Jr. asked to see. The telegram revealed that State Department officials had ordered U.S. diplomats in Europe to stop sending Washington reports about the Nazi mass murder. But DuBois was able to secure a copy of the original telegram and showed it to Morgenthau. Furious at the deception, Morgenthau instructed DuBois to write up a full report exposing the State Department's actions.

On Christmas Day, 1943, DuBois compiled a scathing 18-page memorandum titled "Report to the Secretary on the Acquiescence of This Government in the Murder of the Jews." It concluded that State Department officials "have been guilty not only of gross procrastination and willful failure to act, but even of willful attempts to prevent action from being taken to rescue Jews from Hitler....Unless remedial steps of a drastic nature are taken, and taken immediately...to prevent the complete extermination of the Jews, this Government will have to share for all time responsibility for this extermination."

A BATTLE ON CAPITOL HILL

Meanwhile, the battle for rescue was being waged on other fronts, as well.

Pro-refugee activists known as the Bergson Group placed full-page advertisements in the *New York Times* and other leading newspapers, with headlines such as "They Are Driven to Death Daily--But They Can Be Saved!" and "Time Races Death: What Are We Waiting For?"

Today, it's common for political action groups to sponsor newspaper ads on various issues. But it was not at all common back in the 1940s, so the Bergson Group's ads attracted a great deal of attention. Another reason the ads were important was that many major newspapers did not give prominence to news about the mass killings of the Jews. Refugee advocates used paid advertisements to publicize information that newspaper readers were not seeing on the news pages.

In November 1943, the Bergson Group persuaded members of Congress to introduce a resolution urging the president to create a special government agency to focus on rescue. The Roosevelt administration strongly opposed the resolution, and sent Breckinridge Long to Capitol Hill to testify against it at a hearing before the House Foreign Affairs Committee.

In his testimony Long argued that creating a new agency was unnecessary because the United States was already doing all that was possible to aid the Jews. Among other things, Long claimed that 580,000 Jewish refugees had entered the United States since Hitler's rise to power in 1933.

But that figure was a wild exaggeration. It represented the total number of refugees who theoretically could have received visas

WALLENBERG'S U.S. CONNECTION

One of the War Refugee Board's most important achievements was persuading a young Swedish businessman, Raoul Wallenberg, to undertake a rescue mission in Nazi-occupied Budapest in 1944. With the Board's financing, Wallenberg rescued tens of thousands of Jews. In 1981, he was awarded honorary American citizenship in recognition of his life-saving work.

Raoul Wallenberg

> **PRESIDENTS SPEAK OUT**
>
> Several recent American presidents have criticized the Roosevelt administration's response to the Holocaust.
>
> *Bill Clinton*
>
> President Bill Clinton, speaking at the opening of the U.S. Holocaust Memorial Museum in 1993, said "far too little was done" by the U.S. in response to news of the Holocaust. "Doors to liberty were shut," he noted. "Rail lines to the camps within miles of militarily significant targets were left undisturbed."
>
> *George Bush*
>
> President George W. Bush, after reviewing an exhibit about the failure to bomb Auschwitz at the Yad Vashem Holocaust museum in 2008, remarked, "We should have bombed it."[30]

since 1933, not the number of people who were admitted. The real number of immigrants was less than half of what Long claimed, and not all of them were Jews fleeing persecution. Long's misstatements ignited a firestorm of criticism from Jewish organizations and other refugee advocates.

The criticism of Long, and the front page news coverage of it, escalated in late 1943 and early 1944. With Congress, Jewish groups, the news media, and Treasury Secretary Morgenthau pressing him, FDR finally took action. He demoted Long and established the War Refugee Board, a new government agency whose sole purpose was to rescue Jews from the Holocaust. Although little and late, it represented the first meaningful response by the U.S. government to the Nazi genocide.

Eric Godal
The Answer, June 20, 1943
The style of the uniforms indicates that the first solder is American, the second British, and the third French. Each one tells the refugees to go somewhere else. Note that their final destination is a tombstone, with a Jewish star.

"Refer to Committee 3, Investigation Subcommittee 6, Section 8B, for consideration."

Eric Godal
PM, October 3, 1943

A news article in *PM* on September 29, 1943 began, "One hundred thousand Jews are being killed each month in Poland by the German Government." The article also quoted a statement issued by Jewish leaders in Warsaw shortly before their deaths, in which they criticized the Allies for not acting to rescue European Jewry: "Our Allies must realize at last the full extent of the historic responsibility that will fall upon those who have remained inactive in the face of the Nazis' unparalleled crime against an entire people, the tragic epilogue of which is taking place today." *PM's* cartoonist, Eric Godal, responded with this cartoon.

Beggar: "Please contribute to saving the Jews of Europe!"
FDR: "Excuse me, there must be some mistake. I don't have any relatives in Europe."

There Must Be Some Mistake
Yosef Bass
Ha'aretz, April 13, 1944

This cartoon in the Hebrew-language Palestine newspaper *Ha'aretz* depicts President Roosevelt as indifferent to the suffering of the Jews in Europe.

The Promise Has Been Fulfilled
Yehoshua Adari
HaBoker
July 19, 1944

This cartoon from the Hebrew-language Palestine newspaper *HaBoker* takes direct aim at the claim by Allied leaders that rescue would have to be postponed until military victory was achieved. Jewish organizations argued that if rescue was postponed, there would be no Jews left alive at the end of the war--as this Allied soldier discovers when he arrives to save the Jews. The gravestone is labeled "The Jews of Europe."

"Hey, Jews, we've rescued you!"

38. THE HOLOCAUST RAGES ON

Throughout 1943 and 1944, information about the mass murder of Europe's Jews continued to reach the West and appeared in the press, although usually in the back pages.

Some cartoons referred to the victims as Jews. Some listed the Jews as one among a number of peoples brutalized by the Nazis. And some used euphemisms such as "the little peoples of all Europe." Likewise, a number of other cartoons during these years referred to the victims as "racial minorities," "religious minorities," or " political refugees" rather than as Jews.

Polish Jews being rounded up by the Nazis.

These differences in terminology illustrate the division of opinion among those who were sympathetic to the plight of Europe's Jews. Some believed that since the Jews had been singled out by the Nazis as the only people slated for complete annihilation, and were suffering far more than other occupied peoples in Europe, that fact should be made clear. Others, however, thought that it would be easier to attract public sympathy if the identity of the victims was blurred, or if it seemed that many people were suffering, not just the Jews.

THE UNMENTIONABLE JEWS

Explaining its plans for the 1943 Bermuda refugee conference, the State Department emphasized that "the refugee problem should not be considered as being confined to persons of any particular race or faith." Alexander Uhl, who covered the conference for the New York City newspaper *PM*, reported that the delegates were all taking the same position: "It was regarded as almost improper to mention the word 'Jews.'"

Likewise, the U.S. Office of War Information instructed its staff to avoid mentioning that Jews were the primary victims of Nazi atrocities, because it would be "confused and misleading if it appears to be simply affecting the Jewish people."

A meeting of the American, British, and Soviet foreign ministers in Moscow in October 1943 issued a statement threatening postwar punishment for Nazi war crimes against conquered populations. It mentioned "French, Dutch, Belgian or Norwegian hostages ...Cretan peasants ... the people of Poland," but not Europe's Jews.

Allied officials consistently downplayed the victims' Jewishness because they feared that public recognition of the Jews' unique plight would lead to increased pressure on the Allied governments to take steps they did not want to take, such as admitting more Jewish refugees to the United States, or opening Palestine to Jews fleeing from the Nazis.[38]

Running Short of Jews
Arthur Szyk
PM, July 20, 1943
Standing next to Hitler is Gestapo chief Heinrich Himmler; seated at the end of the table is Propaganda Minister Joseph Goebbels; across from Hitler is Hermann Goering, head of the German air force, the Luftwaffe.

To Be Shot As Dangerous Enemies of the Third Reich!
Arthur Szyk
PM, December 14, 1943

**The Little Peoples of
All Europe**
Jay Darling
New York Herald Tribune
October 21, 1943

Time and Blood Are Running Out
Stan MacGovern
New York Post, April 10, 1944
The British White Paper policy, enacted in May 1939, prevented all but a trickle of Jewish immigration to British-ruled Palestine.

How's Business, Partner?
Eric Godal
PM, January 31, 1944
Hitler wears a butcher's smock. The block on which his axe rests lists the conquered peoples whom the Nazis were persecuting. Hitler's ally, Japanese emperor Hirohito, holds a sword bearing the names of victims of atrocities by the Japanese Army: the people of China and the Philippines, which were occupied by Japan during World War II; and English (British) and American soldiers who were captured by the Japanese.

"But I invented you to crush all the inferior peoples!"

Frankenstein's Monster
Eric Godal
PM, July 24, 1944
Gestapo chief Heinrich Himmler is depicted as a new version of Frankenstein's monster (a story that was also set in Germany), slaughtering Jews and other innocent people throughout Europe and then turning on his Nazi creators.

"Who, Me?"

Who, Me?
Eric Godal
PM, November 27, 1944

39. HUNTING JEWS

Hermann Goering was founder and first commander of the Gestapo, the vicious Nazi secret police, as well as chief of the German air force, the Luftwaffe. He also held numerous other minor offices and titles for his amusement or profit. An avid hunter, he was especially pleased to be named by Hitler, in January 1934, as "Reich Master of the Forest and Hunt."

During a pogrom in Berlin the following year, German mobs pulled Jewish passersby out of their cars and brutally beat them. *Time* magazine called the episode "the most savage Jew hunt since those which immediately followed Adolf Hitler's elevation to power [in 1933] ..." *Time* characterized the attackers as "Jew hunters."

Hermann Goering meets with German pilots.

During the genocide years (1941-1945), the term "Jew hunt" *(Judenjagd,* in German) became the common nickname for operations in which Gestapo agents or police battalions methodically searched specific areas for Jews in hiding. Often these missions would be conducted in the aftermath of mass deportations, to capture those who eluded the initial roundups. Those who were caught were quickly executed, sometimes after being tortured.

The Germans devoted significant resources to these operations, although they involved substantial manpower and relatively few victims. One police veteran later said that his unit took part in such 'hunts' so often that they became "more or less our daily bread."

"THEY ARE HERE FOR THE HUNT"

Jan Karski, a courier for the Polish underground, was smuggled into the Warsaw Ghetto in late 1942 to see first-hand the Nazi persecution of the Jews, so that he could bring the information to journalists and political leaders abroad. As he walked the streets, staring in horror at corpses and emaciated children, gunfire suddenly erupted. His guides pulled him into a nearby building. Through a window, Karski could see two members of the Hitler Youth movement. "They are here for the hunt," one of the guides told him.

Karski's biographer writes: "The boys stood in a deserted street, broad smiles on their faces, their blond hair glistening in the sunlight. One had drawn a pistol. His eyes canvassed the surrounding buildings. The other said something that made him laugh. Then the first boy raised his gun and fired. Jan heard the tinkling of broken glass and a moan of pain from an adjoining building. The boy who fired the shot let out a victorious whoop. His fellow 'warrior' congratulat-

> **A UNIQUE SKILL**
>
> Colonel Hans Landa, the Nazi officer who is the main antagonist in Quentin Tarantino's Oscar-nominated film *Inglourious Basterds* (2009), is nicknamed "The Jew Hunter" because of his skill at hunting down Jews who were hiding in German-occupied France.

ed him. It was another successful *Judenjagd*—another 'Jew hunt.' The Hitler Youth turned and strolled serenely away."[39]

Karski reached England in November 1942. British government officials were interested in hearing his report on political affairs in occupied Europe and the activities of the Polish underground. They were less interested in hearing about the plight of the Jews. Foreign Minister Anthony Eden told Karski that Prime Minister Winston Churchill was too busy to see him. Polish president-in-exile Wladyslaw Raczkiewicz, after meeting with Karski in London, sent a message to Pope Pius XII, asking him to speak out against the Nazi killings. Six weeks later, the pope replied by sending a note saying he had already done all he could for the Jews. Karski's meetings with journalists, however, did generate a series of reports in the British press and on BBC Radio about the slaughter of the Jews.

Karski traveled to the United States in the spring of 1943. His meeting with Supreme Court Justice Felix Frankfurter was a disappointment. Apparently unable to absorb the information Karski brought, Frankfurter told him: "Mr. Karski, I am unable to believe you." On July 28, Karski met with President Franklin Roosevelt, in the White House, for more than an hour. As Karski described the activities of the Polish underground, the president listened with evident interest. FDR also offered advice--he suggested putting skis on small airplanes and having couriers fly them from England to Poland during the wintertime, to bring messages back and forth. But when Karski related details of the mass killings of the Jews, FDR had nothing to say. President Roosevelt viewed the suffering of the Jews as just another unfortunate aspect of what civilians suffer in every war. He did not believe it was justified for the U.S. to use its resources to rescue Jews from the Nazis. As Karski departed, he asked the president what message FDR would like him to bring back to Poland. Roosevelt replied, "Tell your nation we shall win this war."

Goering is Named Master of the Hunt
Carl Rose
Jewish Daily Bulletin
January 28, 1934

Gestapo founder Hermann Goering portrayed not merely as chief of the hunt but as one of the hunting dogs himself.

184

40. THE HOLOCAUST REACHES HUNGARY

On March 19, the Germans occupied Hungary. The last major Jewish community in Europe that had been untouched by the Holocaust, 800,000 in number, was now within Hitler's grasp.

Hungarian Jews were immediately terrorized and abused by the Nazis. Teenager Madeline Deutsch recalled SS men and Hungarian police robbing Jews at gunpoint: "Everybody took off their jewelry and money, whatever money was in the pockets, and everybody placed them in the buckets and the barrels." A few people absentmindedly neglected to hand over something, "and these people were taken and lined up against the wall to be shot later. Among them was my father....They found a small amount, like a dollar bill, in one of his little vest pockets....This is my 14th birthday, and my father was to be shot in front of my eyes momentarily....But apparently they—the SS and the gendarmes and the police—were not given orders yet to kill, [just] to use the worst scare techniques on us so that we would follow orders [and] after several hours they released all these people that were lined up against the wall. [So] it was one of the happiest moments of my life, because my father wasn't to be killed."

Hungarian Jews being deported to Auschwitz.

Within weeks, Jews living outside the major cities, including Madeline's family, were forcibly relocated to makeshift ghettos. Madeline recalled how SS men and their Hungarian allies "came to our homes very early in the morning at dawn and knocking real hard, [shouting] 'Jews, get out of your house. Get out and line up in front of the house.' We couldn't imagine what was happening. I mean it was just a horrible, horrible thing. The children were screaming, and all of us were—were afraid...We were allowed back to the house for just a few minutes to get a little suitcase or a little handbag in which we could put a—a change of clothing and maybe some food, just dry food like a piece of bread [and] then we were being marched down the streets where there was the small ghetto."

THE WHOLE WORLD WAS WATCHING

The ghettos were brutally overcrowded. Food, water, and medicine were scarce. After several weeks, the ghettos were emptied as the Nazis began the mass deportation of Hungarian Jews to the Auschwitz death camp. This chapter of the Holocaust was carried out in full view of the world. "Jews in Hungary Fear Annihilation," read the headline of a report in the *New York Times*, five days before the deportations began, warning that the Germans were "about to start the extermination" of Hungary's Jews, who would be killed by "gas chamber baths" and other methods. Three days after the deportations began, a *Times* article headlined "Savage Blows Hit Jews in Hungary" began: "The first act in a program of mass extermination of Jews in Hungary is over, and 80,000 Jews of the Carpathian provinces have already disappeared. They have been sent to murder camps in Poland."

Throughout June, the U.S. government's War Refugee Board orchestrated a series of public statements by Allied officials, the International Red Cross, the Vatican, and others, urging the Hungarian government to stop cooperating in the deportations. At the same time, Hungarian intelligence intercepted a plea sent by Jewish rescue activists to Allied diplomats, urging the bombing of the railway lines leading from Hungary to Auschwitz.

Shortly afterwards, an Allied bombing raid in the area coincidentally struck one of those lines, convincing Hungarian officials that the Allies were taking military action to aid the Jews. As a result of these developments, Hungarian leader Miklos Horthy announced on July 7 that his government would no longer take part in the deportations. By then, more than 400,000 Hungarian Jews had been deported, but more than 200,000 residing in Budapest were temporarily safe.

A FLOOD OF REFUGEES

On July 18, the Horthy regime informed the British that all Jews holding entry visas for other countries, including Palestine, would be allowed to emigrate. British officials told the Roosevelt administration they would agree to issue a joint statement accepting Horthy's offer, so long as it was privately understood that London was not agreeing to any specific number of immigrants to Palestine. The British were afraid there would be "a flood of refugees," as the Colonial Office put it. After nearly a month of wrangling, the two governments accepted the offer, but as it turned out, the Germans were not prepared to let Jews leave Hungary.

The most the British were willing to provide were 5,000 fake visas, which Jewish leaders hoped would help protect some Jews from immediate deportation. In the past, some Jews holding foreign citizenship or visas to other countries were kept alive by the Germans in the belief they might be later exchanged for German POWs held by the Allies.

In August, the Germans overthrew the Horthy government and replaced it with a regime headed by the fascist and antisemitic Arrow Cross party. The Jews in Budapest were subjected to random violence, and the possibility of renewed deportations seemed real. But Raoul Wallenberg, a Swedish rescue activist in Budapest financed by the War Refugee Board, intervened to provide Jews with protective documents and shelter them in safe houses that he set up. Wallenberg was assisted by a number of foreign diplomats in the city. As a result, more than 100,000 Jews in Budapest survived until the Soviets liberated Hungary from the Nazis in February 1945.[40]

Sorry, My Hands are Tied
Stan MacGovern
New York Post, August 10, 1944
The gentleman with the bowler hat and sideburns is John Bull, the British equivalent of Uncle Sam. Great Britain, represented by the John Bull character, claims that he cannot reach the Palestine visas in his own pocket. His "hands are tied" by a ribbon or rope labeled "delay," but it hangs loose around his hands and could be discarded at any time if he wanted.

What Will We Do About the Other 480,000?
A. W. MacKenzie
New York Post, August 19, 1944
Some news reports claimed the British were considering granting 20,000 visas for Hungarian Jews to go to Palestine. Cartoonist A. W. MacKenzie pointed out that such an offer, even if true, would only help a very small portion of the 500,000 Jews in Nazi-occupied Hungary.

41. "FREE PORTS" FOR CANS OF BEANS —AND FOR PEOPLE

Jewish refugees arriving at the Oswego, NY, shelter, 1944.

In the spring of 1944, the War Refugee Board (WRB) began urging President Roosevelt to create "temporary havens of refuge" in the United States for Jews fleeing Hitler. Since the refugees' status would be similar to that of prisoners of war, they could be admitted outside America's tight immigration quotas. According to the Board's proposal, the refugees would agree to leave the United States after the war ended. This was meant to address the public's fear that America would be flooded with Europe's downtrodden.

"It is essential that we and our allies convince the world of our sincerity and our willingness to bear our share of the burden," WRB general counsel Josiah E. DuBois, Jr. pleaded in a memo to the president. The United States could not reasonably ask countries bordering Nazi-occupied territory, such as Spain and Switzerland, to take in refugees if America itself would not take any, DuBois argued.

FDR was nervous about public opposition to immigration and hesitated to embrace the plan. Secretary of War Henry Stimson vigorously opposed DuBois's proposal. Stimson argued that Jewish refugees were "unassimilable" and would negatively affect America's "racial stock."

CASES OF BEANS

Hoping to whip up public support for the plan, the WRB tipped off newspaper columnist Samuel Grafton that the proposal had stalled. In April 1944, Grafton authored three articles advocating what he called "Free Ports for Refugees."

"A 'free port' is a small bit of land...into which foreign goods may be brought without paying customs duties...for temporary storage," Grafton explained. "Why couldn't we have a system of free ports for refugees fleeing the Hitler terror?...We do it for cases of beans...it should not be impossible to do it for people."

Grafton's catchy slogan and straight-from-the-hip reasoning gave the DuBois plan the crucial publicity that it needed. His columns were syndicated by the *New York Post* and appeared in 40 other newspapers across the country, with a combined circulation of more than four million. The articles generated numerous sympathetic editorials in major newspapers and magazines, and helped win public endorsements from prominent religious, civic, and labor organizations, including the Federal Council of Churches, the American Federation of Labor, the national board of the YWCA (Young Women's Christian Association), and the National Farmers Union.

With pressure mounting, White House aides commissioned a Gallup poll, which found 70 percent of Americans approved of emergency refugee camps in the United States. Yet President Roosevelt was still undecided.

A TOKEN REFUGE

On May 11, War Refugee Board director John Pehle personally showed the president a thick folder of newspaper editorials and articles sympathetic to the free ports idea. It was clear that public opinion was turning in favor of providing haven. FDR eventually agreed to admit one group of 982 Jewish refugees.

The refugees, most of them women and children, arrived in August 1944 aboard the S.S. *Henry Gibbins,* one of the many U.S. troop supply ships that usually returned empty after delivering their cargo to American troops in Europe. Ivo Lederer, one of the passengers, recalled how they cheered when the ship approached the Statue of Liberty in the New York harbor: "If you're coming from wartime, war-damaged Europe to see this enormous sight, lower Manhattan and the Statue of Liberty—I don't think there was a dry eye on deck."

The refugees were taken to Fort Ontario, an abandoned army camp in the upstate New York town of Oswego. The town's residents generally gave them a friendly reception. Moved by the sight of the refugees upon their arrival, one local teenager, Geraldine Rossiter, organized her friends into a human pyramid so she could pass her bicycle over the fence to the refugee children.

Adjusting to life in the Oswego camp was difficult for the refugees, especially after what they had suffered in Europe. Many had lost loved ones or suffered permanent injuries at the hands of their Nazi tormentors. Still, most were able to "find peace," in the words of Rolf Manfred, who was 17 when he arrived. Noting the deep sense of gratitude that the refugees felt for America, Manfred many years later recalled how he still gets "goose bumps" when he sees an American flag or hears "God Bless America" being sung. (After the war, the Truman administration agreed to let the refugees go to Canada and from there re-enter the United States, on a permanent basis, under the regular immigration quotas.)

Sadly, Fort Ontario was the only "free port" in America for Jewish refugees. By contrast, Sweden, which was one-twentieth the size of the United States, took in 8,000 Jews fleeing from Nazi-occupied Denmark. Journalist I.F. Stone criticized the meager U.S. contribution to refugee relief as "a kind of token payment to decency, a bargain-counter flourish in humanitarianism."[41]

A GESTURE OF KINDNESS

Visitors to the Safe Haven Museum, on the site of the former refugee camp in Oswego, NY, can view a videotape of one of the refugees later recalling his arrival at the camp, when he was a teenager: "I had an American dime that I had earned doing odd jobs at an Allied base in Italy just before we got on the boat to come to America. As we were walking into the camp, there was a chain link fence on one side, and I saw some teenage girls watching us. I went over to them and gave one of them the dime, and asked her, in my broken English, if she would please buy me a soda in the grocery store across the street. A few minutes later, she came back with some of her friends, and their arms were filled with bags of potato chips, cookies, cakes, bottles of soda, all kinds of treats. I was amazed at how much you could buy in America for just a dime!"

A couple is reunited at the fence outside the Oswego refugee camp.

Give Them This Haven
Charles Werner
Chicago Sun, May 5, 1944
The possibility of haven in the United States would be like the dawn of a new day, and a new life, for Jewish refugees fleeing Hitler.

Sweet Land of Liberty
Stan MacGovern
New York Post, June 3, 1944
The title of this cartoon is taken from the song "My Country, 'Tis of Thee" (also known as "America"). For cartoonist Stan MacGovern, President Roosevelt's willingness to grant haven to some refugees fulfilled the ideals of liberty and justice articulated in the song.

42. WHAT KIND OF PEACE?

As World War II approached its end, officials within the Roosevelt administration began debating what peace terms the Allies should impose upon Germany and its partners once they were defeated.

The State Department and War Department preferred a "soft peace" that would enable Germany to rebuild quickly. In their view, the German nation as a whole should not be punished and only a small number of prominent Nazis should be prosecuted for war crimes (the persecution of civilians during war time). In addition, the Allies should provide substantial aid to get Germany back on its feet. Presumably this would benefit the economic health of Europe and encourage Germany to side with the United States against the Soviet Union in the postwar period. Assistant Secretary of War John McCloy drew up a handbook for U.S. military officials in Europe, directing them to tread lightly on the Germans.

German soldiers at the Dachau concentration camp surrendering to Allied troops.

PREVENTING WORLD WAR III

Secretary of the Treasury Henry Morgenthau, Jr., supported by General Dwight Eisenhower, Supreme Commander of the Allied Forces in Europe, countered with a tougher proposal, called "Program to Prevent Germany from Starting World War III." Popularly known as the Morgenthau Plan, it proposed to completely demilitarize Germany, divide it into districts, place its major industries under international control, and compel it to become an agriculture-centered society. Germany's education system and news media would be shut down until they could be completely rid of all Nazi-era influences. This, Morgenthau, believed, was the only way to ensure the Germans would not eventually provoke yet another world war.

McCloy and Secretary of War Henry Stimson tried hard to convince President Roosevelt of the wisdom of a "soft peace." They tried to discredit Morgenthau by arguing that he was driven by a Jewish desire to get revenge against the Germans for their treatment of his fellow Jews. Stimson called the Morgenthau Plan "semitism gone wild for vengeance." McCloy claimed Morgenthau was motivated by the fact that "his racial position was affronted by the activities of the Hitler regime."

ROOSEVELT BACKS OFF

In September 1944, details of the controversy began reaching the press. There was some public support for Morgenthau's plan, including from those who believed that the scale of German atrocities showed that a "soft peace" was not justified. But there was also much criticism of the Morgenthau Plan, and President Franklin Roosevelt, who had initially supported Morgenthau's proposal, began backing away from it.

Harry S. Truman became president following President Roosevelt's sudden passing in April 1945, just one month before the defeat of Germany. Truman at first imposed some restrictions on German industries, approved the prosecution of a large number of war criminals, and instituted a "denazification" program intended to rid German society of Nazi influences. But with the Cold War beginning and the U.S. anxious to have Germany on its side against the Soviet Union, the Truman administration soon eased up on those policies. Many Nazi war criminals were pardoned, the denazification process was handed over to local German officials who tended to be extremely lenient, and Germany was permitted to rapidly rebuild its heavy industries.[42]

The Weight of Evidence
Roy Justus
Minneapolis Star, December 1, 1944
Hitler hopes that the Allies will go easy on Germany in the aftermath of the war—but in the cartoonist's view, the enormous evidence of Nazi atrocities against the Jews will make a compelling case for a firm Allied policy on punishing the Nazis for their war crimes.

43. JUDGEMENT DAY

Soon after the United States entered World War II, the Roosevelt administration began planning for the arrest and postwar prosecution of Nazi war criminals. Even at that early stage, the Allies knew enough about Nazi atrocities against Jews and others to know that, if and when they won the war, they would have many war criminals on their hands. Yet U.S. policy on what to do with those war criminals was ambivalent.

Nazi leaders on trial for war crimes, at Nuremberg.

In 1942, President Roosevelt publicly pledged that Nazi war criminals would be punished. The following year, the Allies established a United Nations War Crimes Commission. But the State Department wanted to limit postwar trials to only the most prominent and notorious war criminals, for fear that prosecuting large numbers of Germans could harm America's relations with Germany after the war.

The U.S. representative to the war crimes commission, Herbert C. Pell, favored prosecuting all Nazi war criminals. That brought him into repeated conflicts with State Department officials, who tried to undermine Pell's work.

Pell had been appointed to his new post in June 1943, but it was not until November that the State Department finally cleared him to travel to the meetings of the war crimes commission, in London. In addition, State would not let Pell bring Harvard law professor Sheldon Glueck to London as his legal adviser, insisting that the State Department's own man, Lawrence Preuss, accompany him.

Preuss soon sparked an uproar at the London meetings by openly opposing Pell's proposal to prosecute all war criminals. Preuss also tried to sabotage Pell by secretly sending Washington harshly critical reports about Pell's work in London.

On a visit to the U.S. in late 1944 to attend the wedding of his son Claiborne—a future U.S. Senator from Rhode Island—Pell met with President Roosevelt at the White House for a friendly chat. The president did not mention that he had already privately agreed to the State Department's request to dump Pell. A few hours later, the State Department informed Pell that his service had been terminated because it could no longer find $30,000 in its budget to fund his position. Pell promptly offered to work for free; State replied that it would be illegal for him to work without being paid.

JUSTICE, NOT REVENGE

Pell turned to the Emergency Committee to Save the Jewish People of Europe (the Bergson Group) to help him publicize the scandal. At a press conference in New York City organized by the Emergency Committee in January 1945, Pell blew the story wide open. He urged punishment of "every Gestapo member who has caused suffering," denounced the State Department for leaving his proposals "to gather dust in the files of its legal adviser," and labeled as "nonsense" the State Department's explanations for his termination. "If we are not tough and hard toward the war criminals," he explained, "it will encourage other tyrants to try the same thing—to murder, persecute and loot from minorities. Conviction and punishment of Axis war criminals is not a matter of revenge. It is justice."

The Pell scandal appeared on the front page of the *New York Times* and throughout the American press. Embarrassed by the avalanche of negative publicity, the State Department was forced to reconsider its position. Within days, Acting Secretary of State Joseph Grew announced a complete reversal of its previous position: the State Department now agreed that Nazi murderers of European Jews should be prosecuted.

PARDONS FOR KILLERS

Twenty-four of the most prominent war criminals were put on trial by the Allies in a series of military tribunals in the German city of Nuremberg in 1945-1946. Nineteen were convicted, of whom twelve were sentenced to death.

Twelve additional trials, of lesser-known war criminals, were held between 1946 and 1949. Of those 185 defendants, 142 were convicted. But as time went on, the United States showed less and less interest in bringing war criminals to trial. And many of those who had been convicted and jailed were soon set free, thanks to John McCloy, who became U.S. High Commissioner for Germany in 1949. One hundred and four German industrialists were convicted of war crimes, and 84 were still in jail when McCloy arrived in Germany. Of those 84, McCloy reduced the sentences of 74 to time already served, thus setting them free immediately.[43]

John J. McCloy

Witnesses for the Prosecution
Daniel Fitzpatrick
St. Louis Post-Dispatch, April 30, 1945

Last Chapter of Mein Kampf
Daniel Fitzpatrick
St. Louis Post-Dispatch, June 8, 1945

As a Nazi war criminal faces justice, his hands drip with the blood of his victims.

Higher and Higher
Roy Justus
Minneapolis Star, April 14, 1945

Closed
Vaughn Shoemaker
Chicago Daily News, May 4, 1945
The hand labeled "Allies" is bandaged, alluding to the losses suffered by the Allies during the world war. The end of the war and the Allies' defeat of the Nazis has "closed" Hitler's blood-soaked book, *Mein Kampf,* which rests on the skulls of his victims. But did the end of World War II and the Holocaust close the book on future racism, discrimination, and persecution? Will future generations learn the lessons from that terrible era?

ABOUT THE CARTOONISTS

Adari, Yehoshua (1911 – 1966) left his native Poland in 1932 to settle in British Mandatory Palestine. He was the staff cartoonist for Hebrew language daily newspapers such as *HaYarden, HaMashkif,* and *HaBoker.*

Bass, Yosef (1908 – 1995) grew up in Poland and contributed editorial cartoons to various Polish publications. In the face of rising antisemitism in interwar Poland, Bass and his family immigrated to British Mandatory Palestine in 1936. For more than thirty years, he contributed a weekly political cartoon to *Ha'aretz,* a leading Hebrew-language daily, while also emerging as a major figure in Israeli theatrical design. Eleven volumes of his collected cartoons were published in Israel between 1942 and 1980.

Berg, R.O. A cartoonist who frequently targeted prejudice against both Jews and African-Americans, R. O. Berg was published regularly in *The Crisis,* a magazine published by the National Association for the Advancement of Colored People (NAACP) in the early 1930s.

Block, Herbert (1909 – 2001), popularly known by his signature "Herblock," began his career as a political cartoonist in 1933 with the Newspaper Enterprise Association, and won his first Pulitzer Prize in 1942. From 1946 until his death in 2001, he served as chief editorial cartoonist for the *Washington Post,* during which time he won the Pulitzer twice more, in 1954 and 1979. Block was a particularly fierce critic of Senator Joseph McCarthy, and in fact coined the term "McCarthyism" in a 1950 cartoon. Vice President Richard Nixon famously canceled his subscription to the *Post* after a particularly biting Herblock cartoon about him in 1954. Block was awarded the Presidential Medal of Freedom in 1994.

Burck, Jacob (1907 – 1982) came to America from Poland as a child and attended the Cleveland School of Art, reportedly receiving a scholarship after a faculty member spotted him drawing on a sidewalk. In the late 1920s, Burck became a cartoonist for the Communist Party USA's daily newspaper, *The Daily Worker,* and its monthly magazine, *The New Masses.* Commissioned to create a series of murals in Moscow in 1935-1936, Burck left without completing the project when the authorities insisted he alter the artwork to glorify Soviet dictator Josef Stalin. In 1938, Burck became the editorial cartoonist for the *Chicago Times,* where he remained for the rest of his career. He won the Pulitzer Prize for cartooning in 1941.

Cargill, Jesse T. (1892 – 1967) After studying at the Academy of Fine Arts in Chicago, Cargill spent three years at the *Kansas City Journal* in the 1920s, before settling in as a staff cartoonist for the Central Press Association, a subsidiary of the King Features Syndicate.

Carmack, Paul R. (1895 – 1977), a graduate of the Art Institute of Chicago, was an editorial cartoonist for the *Christian Science Monitor* from 1925 until 1961. He also created and drew the *Monitor's* popular children's comic Strip, *The Diary of Snubs, Our Dog.*

Cassel, John (1877 – 1960) was an editorial cartoonist for the *Brooklyn Eagle* and *the New York World.* His cartoons also appeared in the NAACP's magazine, *The Crisis.*

Charlot, Louis Henri Jean (1898 – 1979), a French painter and illustrator, came to the United States in the 1930s to create murals for the U.S. government's Federal Arts Project, while also occasionally contributing cartoons and illustrations to various American publications, including *Commonweal.* He later headed the art school of the Colorado Springs Fine Arts Center, and taught at the University of Hawaii for more than 30 years.

Darling, Jay (1876 – 1962) was popularly known as "Ding," the name he used to sign his artwork. An Iowa native, Darling served as the editorial cartoonist for the *Des Moines Register and Leader.* Darling's work was also published in the *New York Herald Tribune* from 1917 to 1949. He won the Pulitzer Prize in 1924 and again in 1943. An active conservationist, he created the Federal Duck Stamp program to protect wetland habitats. He was chosen by President Franklin Roosevelt to head the U.S. Biological Survey, which later became the U.S. Fish and Wildlife Service.

Doyle, Jerry (1898 – 1986) was the editorial cartoonist for the *Philadelphia Record* from 1928 to 1947. Among Doyle's most ardent fans was President Franklin Roosevelt, who reportedly owned one of the largest collections of original Doyle cartoons.

Dr. Seuss, see Geisel, Theodor.

Duffy, Edmund (1899 – 1962), the longtime editorial cartoonist for the *Baltimore Sun*, was a three-time Pulitzer laureate. The newspaper's editor, H.L. Mencken, once said of Duffy, "Give me a good cartoonist and I can throw out half the editorial staff."

Elderman, Henry "Gene" (1910 – 1963) served as editorial cartoonist for the *Washington Post* from 1932 to 1942. He left the *Post* in 1942 to serve in World War II, even though he was already in his 30s, and became a cartoonist for *Victory magazine*, published by the U.S. Office of War Information.

Ellis, Fred C. (1885 – 1965) A former teenage office boy for famed architect Frank Lloyd Wright, Fred Ellis worked as a trucker for a meat factory in order to earn enough money to enroll himself in the Chicago Academy of Fine Arts. That work experience, including the turmoil of an unsuccessful strike, radicalized Ellis's political perspective and paved the way for much of his subsequent career. During a lengthy convalescence from work injuries suffered in 1919, Ellis refined his artistic skills and began drawing cartoons for radical-left publications such as *The New Masses*. By 1927, he was the staff cartoonist for the Communist Party USA's newspaper, *The Daily Worker*.

Fitzpatrick, Daniel (1891 – 1969), a graduate of the Chicago Art Institute, drew briefly for the *Chicago Daily News* before settling in at the *St. Louis Post-Dispatch*, where he was the editorial cartoonist from 1913 to 1958. He won the Pulitzer Prize for his editorial cartoons in 1926 and 1954.

Fraydas, Stan (1908 – 1985), a Belgian who graduated from the Royal Academy of Fine Arts in Brussels, immigrated to the United States in 1940. His cartoons appeared in the *Saturday Evening Post, Collier's, Life,* and many other publications.

Gale, Edmund W. (1884 – 1975) was born in Kentucky and settled in Los Angeles as a child. After graduating from high school, he taught himself to draw cartoons. Gale worked for the *Los Angeles Evening News*. He became the editorial cartoonist for the *Los Angeles Times* from 1907 to 1934, when he switched to its competitor, the *Los Angeles Examiner*.

Geisel, Theodor (1904 – 1991), better known by his pen name "Dr. Seuss," grew up in Springfield, Massachusetts, near Mulberry Street, later the subject of his famous children's book *And to Think That I Saw It on Mulberry Street!* Originally an illustrator for advertisements, Seuss began contributing editorial cartoons to *PM* in 1940. After World War II, he moved to California, where he created world-famous children's books such as *The Cat in the Hat* (1957), *How the Grinch Stole Christmas* (1957), and *Green Eggs and Ham* (1960).

Godal, Eric (1889 – 1958) was a Jewish refugee from Nazi Germany. Born Erich Goldman, Godal was a political cartoonist for various publications, especially the New York City daily newspaper *PM*, and drew cartoons and covers for *Collier's* magazine. He was also an oil painter and illustrated books for both adults and children.

Gropper, William (1897 – 1977) was the son of East European Jewish immigrants working in New York City's garment industry. Gropper is said to have turned to radical politics partly as the result of the death of a favorite aunt in the notorious 1911 Triangle Shirtwaist Factory fire. After graduating from the New York School of Fine and Applied Arts, he became a cartoonist for various communist and pro-communist newspapers and magazines. During the McCarthy era, he was questioned by the House Un-American Activities Committee about his radical ties. After the Holocaust, Gropper devoted one painting each year to an aspect of Jewish life, as a tribute to the victims of Nazism.

Hoffman, Irwin D. (1901 – 1989) was born in Boston, one of four sons of Russian immigrants. A gifted young artist, at 15 he took classes at the Boston Museum of Fine Arts School.

Hutton, Hugh M. (1897 – 1976) A journalist before becoming a cartoonist, Hutton worked for the *Nebraska State Journal* in the 1920s, and then worked as a cartoonist for the United Features syndicate as well as taking on miscellaneous illustrating jobs, including a brief stint as the artist for the *Tarzan* daily comic strip. In 1933, he became the editorial cartoonist for the *Philadelphia Public Ledger* (which later became the *Philadelphia Inquirer*), where he remained for the rest of his career.

Jensen, Cecil (1902 – 1976) The Utah-born Jensen studied at the Academy of Fine Arts in Chicago, before returning to Utah to become the editorial cartoonist of the *Salt Lake Telegram* in the 1920s. Later, he was a cartoonist for the *Los Angeles News* and then the *Chicago Daily News*.

Johnstone, Will B. (1883 – 1944) An alumnus of the Chicago Art Institute, Johnstone was a staff cartoonist for the *New York World Telegram* for much of his career. He is best known as the creator of the "taxpayer" cartoon character, who wore only a barrel and suspenders (to symbolize how the tax authorities had taken away all his money and possessions, leaving him with nothing but a barrel). Johnstone was also an accomplished songwriter (his credits include the Prohibition Era ditty, "How Dry I Am") and playwright. He authored the Marx Brothers' first Broadway show, *I'll Say She Is*, and co-wrote some of their later Hollywood films.

Justus, Roy B. (1901 – 1983) A South Dakota native, Justus first came to public attention by drawing cartoons on the window of a local drugstore. He broke into the cartooning business in 1924, with the *Sioux City Tribune*, working there, and for its successor, the *Sioux City Journal*, for the next twenty years. From 1944 until 1975, he was the editorial cartoonist of the *Minneapolis Star*.

Kirby, Rollin (1875-1952) was the first American cartoonist to win a Pulitzer Prize for cartooning, receiving that honor in 1921, 1924, and 1928. After studying art in Paris and New York, Kirby worked for a time as an illustrator for *Collier's*, *Harper's*, and other magazines. He began his editorial cartooning for the *New York Mail* and *New York Sun*, then moved to the *New York World* in 1913 and remained there for most of his career. An active proponent of women's suffrage, Kirby contributed cartoons to numerous women's rights publications.

Limbach, Russell T. (1904 – 1971) After studying at the Cleveland School of Art in the 1920s, Limbach rose to prominence as a lithographer. At the same time, he drew editorial cartoons for communist publications such as *The Daily Worker* and *The New Masses*. Limbach also played an important role in the Roosevelt administration's Public Works of Art Project. Beginning in 1941, he served on the faculty of Wesleyan University, in Connecticut.

Low, David (1891 – 1963) A cartoonist for newspapers in New Zealand and Australia as a teenager, Low moved to England in 1919 and soon became one of the country's most prominent political cartoonists, first with the *Evening Standard* (1927-1949), then the *Daily Herald* (1950-1953), and finally the *Manchester Guardian* (1953-1963). As a result of his cartoons lampooning Hitler and Mussolini, Low's work was banned in Nazi Germany and fascist Italy, and German officials reportedly urged the British government, in 1937, to pressure Low to change his political line (he refused). Low characterized himself as "a nuisance dedicated to sanity." He was knighted in 1962.

MacGovern, Stan (1903 – 1975) drew assorted cartoon features for a number of newspapers beginning in the 1920s, the most successful of which was the comic strip *Silly Milly*. He also occasionally contributed editorial cartoons to the *New York Post*.

MacKenzie, A.W. was a prolific editorial cartoonist who lived in Maplewood, New Jersey, and worked for the *New York Post* and the *New York Mirror* from the early 1930s to the late 1940s.

Milians, Max P. (1907 – 2005) was the staff cartoonist for the *Daily Argus*, in Mount Vernon, New York. He also chaired the National Cartoonists Council's efforts to raise public awareness about infantile paralysis. At the age of 85, Milians received the Simon Rockower Award from the American Jewish Press Association for Excellence in Editorial Cartooning.

Navon, Arie (1909 – 1996) The Russian-born Navon moved to Palestine as a child. He served as the editorial cartoonist for the Hebrew-language daily newspaper *Davar* from 1933 until 1964. Trained as a painter and engraver, Navon became a prominent figure in the Israeli theater industry, designing sets for more than 150 plays over several decades. His stage designs earned him the country's most prestigious award, the Israel Prize, in 1996.

Packer, Fred L. (1886 – 1956) A graduate of the Los Angeles School of Art and Design, Packer was the editorial cartoonist for the *New York Daily Mirror* from 1932 until 1956. During World War II, he drew cartoons and posters for the war effort, and was one of the leaders of Victory Builders, an organization that designed posters for military industries to inspire greater production. Packer won the Pulitzer Prize for cartooning in 1952.

Page, Grover (1893 – 1958), who grew up in North Carolina, is said to have decided at age ten that he was going to be a cartoonist. He made good on his vow, serving as editorial cartoonist for *The Courier-Journal* (of Louisville, Kentucky) for nearly 40 years.

Pergament, Myles Although not a professional cartoonist, Pergament, a member of the Non-Sectarian Anti-Nazi League to Champion Human Rights, often contributed political cartoons to the League's monthly magazine, *The Anti-Nazi Bulletin*. In 1933, the League, which was based in New York City, organized the first boycott in the United States of German-made products.

Rankin, Ainsworth H. "Doc" (1896 – 1954) was a freelance cartoonist who created art for humor books and advertising in the 1920s and 1930s, while at the same time contributing editorial cartoons to the *Brooklyn Eagle*. In 1940, he gave up cartooning for a career in the U.S. Army, eventually reaching the rank of Lieutenant-Colonel.

Reinhardt, Adolf F. (1913 – 1967), who studied art at Columbia University, was a widely-exhibited abstract painter. He also contributed illustrations and editorial cartoons to a range of publications, from the pro-communist *Student Advocate* to the daily *PM*. While serving in the U.S. military in World War II, Reinhardt helped design an anti-racism pamphlet, *Races of Mankind*, which was banned by the army. In his later years, Reinhardt taught at Brooklyn College and other institutions.

Richter, Mischa (1910 – 2001) As a child, Richter fled with his family from the turmoil of the Russian Revolution, settling in the United States in 1922. He studied at Boston's School of the Museum of Fine Arts, as well as at Yale. His cartoon feature, "Strictly Richter," was syndicated by the King Features Syndicate. More than 1,500 of Richter's cartoons—he preferred the term "magazine art"—appeared in *The New Yorker*, beginning in 1942. He also drew cartoons for *Collier's, PM,* the *Saturday Evening Post,* and other publications. Richter was honored by the National Cartoonists Society in 1974 (its Award for Gag Cartoons) and 1979 (its Award for Advertising and Illustration).

ROBINSON, J. PARKER was a freelance cartoonist from Great Britain. During World War II, his work appeared regularly in the *Christian Science Monitor.*

ROSE, CARL (1903 – 1971) first made a name for himself with a 1928 cartoon in the *New Yorker* in which a mother tells her daughter at the dinner table, "It's broccoli, dear," and the girl replies, "I say it's spinach, and I say the hell with it." The cartoon was so popular that it became the subject of a song, "I Say It's Spinach," in a Broadway musical. Rose contributed cartoons to a variety of magazines and newspapers, including a particularly prolific run in the *Jewish Daily Bulletin* in the early 1930s. In 1958, he received the National Cartoonist Society's Advertising and Illustration Award.

RUSSELL, BRUCE A. (1903 – 1963) began as a sports cartoonist for the *Los Angeles Times* in 1927. He gradually worked his way up to becoming chief editorial cartoonist, from 1934 until his death. Russell won the Pulitzer Prize in 1947.

SEIBEL, FRED O. (1886 – 1968), a native of upstate New York, honed his artistic skills sketching the Erie Canal. He began his cartooning career with the Albany (NY) *Knickerbocker Press* and the *Utica Herald-Dispatch*, then served as the editorial cartoonist for the Richmond (Va.) *Times-Dispatch* from 1926 until he retired in 1968.

SHOEMAKER, VAUGHN (1902 – 1991) became editorial cartoonist for the *Chicago Daily News* at the age of 22 and remained there for nearly 30 years. He created the character "John Q. Public" as a symbol of the average American citizen. Shoemaker won the Pulitzer Prize for editorial cartooning in 1938 and 1947.

STRUBE, SIDNEY (1892 – 1956) was the editorial cartoonist for the *London Daily Express* from 1912 to 1948. During many of those years, it had the largest circulation of any newspaper in the world. In part because of Strube's strong anti-Nazi cartoons, the *Express* was banned in Germany under Hitler. After the war, Strube's name was found on a Nazi hit list.

SYKES, CHARLES HENRY "BILL" (1882 – 1942), a graduate of Philadelphia's Drexel Institute, was an editorial cartoonist for *Life* magazine in the 1920s, and then for the *Philadelphia Public Ledger* from 1914 until it ceased publication in 1942. At the time of his death, Sykes, who had smoked four packs of cigarettes daily, was working on a series of anti-smoking advertisements.

SZYK, ARTHUR (1894 – 1951) grew up in Poland but moved to Paris in 1921, where he emerged as a prominent book illustrator and miniaturist. Nervous book publishers in Poland and Czechoslovakia turned down one of Szyk's most famous creations, a Passover haggada with anti-Nazi imagery; it was eventually published by friends in England. Szyk contributed cartoons to the British war effort, then went to the United States in 1940, where he drew anti-Nazi caricatures for *Time, Life,* and other leading magazines, as well as editorial cartoons for *PM* and the *New York Post*. First Lady Eleanor Roosevelt is said to have remarked, "This is a personal war of Szyk against Hitler, and I do not think that Mr. Szyk will lose this war!" Szyk was also active in the Bergson Group, which lobbied for rescue of Jews from the Holocaust and creation of a Jewish state.

TEMPLE, KEITH (1899 – 1980) A native of Australia, Temple was visiting the United States in 1919, when he fell ill and had to be hospitalized in New Orleans. To pay his medical bills, Temple found work as a reporter, then as an artist, at the local newspaper, the *Times-Picayune*. He served as its editorial cartoonist from 1923 until his retirement in 1967. After finding himself the target of a libel suit over one of his cartoons, Temple decided to study law at Loyola University, graduating in 1927.

WERNER, CHARLES (1909 – 1997) was working for the *Daily Oklahoman* when his cartoon "Nomination for 1938," about Nazi Germany's annexation of the Sudetenland, won him the Pulitzer Prize. At 29, he was the youngest artist ever to receive the coveted award. Werner worked for the *Chicago Sun,* the *Indianapolis Star,* and was president of the Association of American Editorial Cartoonists. Presidents Lyndon B. Johnson and Harry Truman both requested Werner's original cartoons. Werner was named one of the world's six best cartoonists by the 1969 International Salon of Cartoons, in Montreal.

WHITE, GEORGE (1901 – 1964) The sports and editorial cartoonist for the *Tampa Tribune* from the 1930s to the 1960s, White was often published on the front page of the *Tribune*. The Associated Press once described White as having an "amalgam of artistic skill and political savvy."

INDEX TO CARTOONISTS

Adari, Yehoshua: 176 (The Promise Fulfilled)

Bass, Yosef: 145 (Letter from Exile); 164 (Non Stop Express to Bermuda); 176 (There Must Be Some Mistake)

Berg, R. O.: 20 (Four Years of the Hitler Wreckord)

Block, Herbert ("Herblock"): 28 (Hail Hitler); 31 (Burnt Offering); 70 (Simplified Finances); 111 ("Light! More Light!"); 115 (Still No Solution); 117 (Civilization Can Do Better); 137 (Tragedy at Sea)

Burck, Jacob: 32 (On the Altars of the Nazis)

C.E.D.: 103 (untitled)

Cargill, Jesse T.: 138 (Rock of Ages, Cleft for Me)

Carmack, Paul R.: 115 (Humanity Mobilizes); 118 (The Best Answer to Race Persecution)

Cassel, John: 67 (A Qualified Valentine)

Charlot, Jean: 120 (Refugees Without Refuge)

Darling, Jay ("Ding"): 18 (A Good Way to Find Out); 90 (All Our Lessons to Do Over Again); 102 (Great Sportsmen); 108 (Meet Our New Epoch); 109 (Germany Isn't the Only Place They're Rough on Minority Groups); 179 (The Little Peoples of All Europe)

Doyle, Jerry: 78 (The Modern Mercury); 100 ("Villain!"); 134 (Another Refugee Ship)

Dr. Seuss (Geisel, Theodor): 55 (Early Mein Kampf); 126 (Adolf the Wolf); 152 (untitled)

Duffy, Edmund: 8 (Maryland, My Maryland); 25 (Germany's Newest Ensign); 27 (A Salute to the World); 43 (The Little Brown [Shirt] Schoolhouse); 59 (The Sower); 63 (The Official Flag on the Old Staff); 83 (Fresh Fields); 84 (The Swastika Spur); 92 (Inferiority Complex); 106 (The Nation Followed its Healthy Instincts); 107 (1215-1938 and All That); 130 (Relativity); 136 (The Wandering Jew); 141 Outstretched Hand)

Elderman, Henry ("Gene"): 110 (My Battle); 122 (Mark of the Beast)

Ellis, Fred: 60 (untitled); 168 (Warsaw Jews)

Fitzpatrick, Daniel R.: 26 (We and They); 62 (Swastika Over Germany); 96 (Exodus, 1938); 118 (No Place to Lay Their Heads); 197 (Witnesses for the Prosecution); 198 (Last Chapter of *Mein Kampf*)

Fraydas, Stan: 154 (News From Abroad)

Edmund W. Gale: 16 (The Watch On the Rhine); 22 (A Throw-back to the Dark Ages!)

Godal, Eric: 38 ("Now This is Going to Hurt Me More Than You!"); 95 (The Wandering Jew); 149 (Internment Camp); 158 (International Exhibition); 174 (untitled); 175 (untitled); 181 (How's Business, Partner?); 182 (Frankenstein's Monster; Who, Me?)

Gropper, William: 77 (Olympic Games)

Hoffman, Irwin D.: 44 (The Patriot Master's Reward)

Hutton, Hugh M.: 112 (Darkness Descends; It's None of Your Business What I Do); 114 (untitled)

Jensen, Cecil: 89 (Next?); 109 (Eclipse); 123 (Mayflower)

Johnstone, Will B.: 56 (Masterpieces)

Justus, Roy B.: 194 (The Weight of Evidence); 199 (Higher and Higher)

Kallaugher, Kevin: 10 (We Need to Borrow a Pen)

Kirby, Rollin: 14 (The Pyromaniac); 70 (Birds of a Feather)

Limbach, Russell T.: 34 (Keeping the Home Fire Burning)

Low, David: 142 *(Lebensraum* for the Conquered); 157 (How the Beastly Business Begins); 162 (Jews to the Slaughter House)

M. W.: 34 (untitled)

MacGovern, Stan: 180 (Time and Blood Are Running Out); 187 (Sorry, My Hands Are Tied); 192 (Sweet Land of Liberty)

MacKenzie, A.W.: 188 (What Will We Do About the Other 480,000?)

Navon, Arie: 166 (Rescuers)

Packer, Fred L.: 135 (Ashamed)

Page, Grover: 101 ("As Ye Would That Men Should Do to You"); 110 ("Go Ahead--Shoot!")

Pergament, Myles: 64 (The New Ten Commandments)

Rankin, Ainsworth H. ("Doc"): 72 (No Regard for the Misery)

Reinhardt, Adolf F. ("Ad"): 47 (Heidelberg)

Richter, Mischa: 37 (International Bankers)

Robinson, J. Parker: 120 (Wanted: A Christian Answer)

Rose, Carl: 19 (The Year One of the Second Coming of the Vandals); 21 (Calvary 1933); 33 (Apotheosis); 36 (The Call to the Pogrom); 38 (The Weeping Crocodile of Franconia); 39 (The Largest Purveyors of Their Line in the World); 40 (The Gospel of a Perfect Aryan); 48 (Post-Graduate Work for German Professors); 50 (The Indictment); 52 (Nazi Concentration Camp); 53 (Nazis Ban Tuberculin for Cattle Because its Discoverer is a Jew); 54 (Can These Restrictions Have Been Overlooked by *Unser* Adolf?); 58 (Victims of the Cold Pogrom Need Your Aid--Give!); 59 (One Despot to Another); 66 (A Little Lesson in Economics); 79 (Hitlerite Sportsmanship); 80 (untitled); 87 (Advice From Hitler's Special Ambassador); 88 (Anschluss); 129 (Germany's "Gifts" to the Nations); 150 (Thru Darkest North Africa); 184 (Goering is Named Master of the Hunt)

Russell, Bruce A.: 71 (Shakedown); 117 (Coming Home with Him!); 124 (There Isn't Any Turkey in Europe)

S.: 74 (untitled)

Seibel, Fred O.: 108 (And This is the Twentieth Century!)

Dr. Seuss (Theodor Geisel): 55 (Mein Early Kampf); 152 (untitled)

Shoemaker, Vaughn: 121 (Nazi Calvary); 124 (Pilgrims are Still Landing); 140 ("Keep Moving!"); 200 (Closed)

Strube, Sidney: 98 (Will the Evian Conference Guide Him to Freedom?)

Sykes, Charles H. : 107 (Back to the Dark Ages); 116 (Beggar on Horseback; The Boomerang Boy)

Szyk, Arthur: 132 (Palestine Restricted); 145 (Enemies of the Third Reich); 146 (Berlin Sportpalast); 161 (Ghouls of Blackness); 160 (Who Cares?); 169 (The Repulsed Attack); 170 (We Will Never Go Back to the Ghetto); 178 (Running Short of Jews); 179 (To Be Shot As Enemies of the Third Reich)

Temple, Keith: 17 (Just in Case He Goosesteps Too Much!); 68 (How Much Will You Pay Me to Stop?); 91 (Does He Really Like It?); 111 (The Secretary of the Treasury Reports)

Werner, Charles: 191 (Give Them This Haven)

White, George: 104 (Inconsistent)

SOURCE NOTES

1 Deborah Lipstadt, *Beyond Belief: The American Press & the Coming of the Holocaust 1933-1945* (New York: Free Press, 1986), pp.14-17.

2 Anne O'Hare McCormick, "Hitler Seeks Jobs for All Germans," *New York Times*, July 10, 1933, p.1.

3 Allert Tilman, *The Nazi Salute*. (New York: Henry Holt and Company, 2008.)

4 Stephen H. Norwood, *The Third Reich in the Ivory Tower: Complicity and Conflict on American Campuses* (New York: Cambridge University Press, 2010), pp.226-28, 241; "Nazis to Purge Vienna Library; 'Non-Aryan' Works to Be Burned," *New York Times*, April 24, 1938, p.1.

5 *Presidential News Conferences of Franklin D. Roosevelt*, Number 142: September 7, 1934, pp.60-61, Franklin D. Roosevelt Presidential Library, Hyde Park, NY

6 Uta Larkey, *Life and Loss in the Shadow of the Holocaust: A Jewish Family's Untold Story* (New York: Cambridge University Press, 2011), pp.68-73.

7 Stephen H. Norwood, *The Third Reich in the Ivory Tower: Complicity and Conflict on American Campuses* (New York: Cambridge University Press, 2010); Arye Carmon, "The Impact of the Nazi Racial Decrees on the University of Heidelberg: A Case Study," *Yad Vashem Studies* 11 (1976), pp.131-41.

8 Dorothy Thompson, "The Record of Persecution," in Pierre Van Paassen and James Waterman Wise, eds., *Nazism: An Assault on Civilization* (New York: Smith & Haas, 1934), p.12; James Waterman Wise, *Swastika: The Nazi Terror* (New York: Smith & Haas, 1933), pp.100-114.

9 Edward I. Koch and Rafael Medoff, "La Guardia and the Holocaust," *Midstream*, March/April 2006, pp.9-13.

10 Laurel Holliday, *Children in the Holocaust and World War II: Their Secret Diaries* (New York: Washington Square Press, 1995), pp.106-107.

11 Jeremy Schaap, *Triumph: The Untold Story of Jesse Owens and Hitler's Olympics* (New York: Houghton Mifflin Harcourt, 2007); Deborah Lipstadt, *Beyond Belief: The American Press & the Coming of the Holocaust 1933 – 1945* (New York: Free Press, 1986), pp.81-84.

12 John V. H. Dippel, *Bound Upon a Wheel of Fire: Why So Many German Jews Made the Tragic Decision to Remain in Nazi Germany* (New York: Basic Books, 1996).

13 Ezra Mendelsohn, *The Jews of East Central Europe between the World Wars* (Bloomington: Indiana University Press, 1983).

14 William L. Shirer, *The Rise and Fall of the Third Reich* (Simon and Schuster, 1960), p.477 and *Berlin Diary: The Journal of a Foreign Correspondent, 1934-1941* (Taylor and Francis, 2002), p.103.

15 David S. Wyman, *Paper Walls: America and the Refugee Crisis 1938-1941* (Amherst, MA: University of Massachusetts Press, 1968); Bat-Ami Zucker, *In Search of Refuge: Jews and U.S. Consuls in Nazi Germany 1933-1941* (New York and London: Vallentine Mitchell, 2001), pp.81-82, 93.

16 *Time*, July 18, 1938, p.16; *Newsweek*, July 18, 1938, p.13; Walter F. Mondale, "Evian and Geneva," *New York Times*, July 28, 1979, p.17; Dennis R. Laffer, "The Jewish Trail of Tears: The Evian Conference of 1938," Ph.D. dissertation, University of South Florida (2011), pp.155, 350.

17 Martin Gilbert, *Kristallnacht: Prelude to Destruction* (New York: Harper Collins, 2007), p.30; Rick Perlmutter, "Floridian Teaches Holocaust 'Close-Up'," *Miami Jewish Tribune*, October 18-24, 1991, p.3.

18 Rafael Medoff, "Christians Mostly Failed to Act in Response to Kristallnacht," *Jewish Telegraphic Agency*, October 31, 2011; Henry L. Feingold, *The Politics of Rescue: The Roosevelt Administration and the Holocaust 1938-1945* (New Brunswick, NJ: Rutgers University Press, 1970), p.150.

19 Andy Marino, *A Quiet American: The Secret War of Varian Fry* (New York: St. Martin's, 1999); Jarrell C. Jackman, *The Muses Flee Hitler: Cultural Transfer and Adaptation, 1930-1945* (Washington, D.C.: Smithsonian Institute, 1983).

20 Sarah A. Ogilvie and Scott Miller, *Refuge Denied: The St. Louis Passengers and the Holocaust* (Madison, WI: University of Wisconsin Press, 2010).

21 Sigrid Schultz, *Germany Will Try It Again* (New York: Reynal and Hitchcock, 1944), pp.185-86.

22 A. Anatoli (Kuznetsov), *Babi Yar: A Document in the Form of a Novel* (New York: Farrar, Strauss and Giroux, 1970).

23 Andrew Ezergailis, *The Holocaust in Latvia 1941-1944* (Riga, Latvia: The Historical Institute of Latvia, 1996), pp.257-58.

24 Michael Abitbol, *The Jews of North Africa During the Second World War* (Detroit: Wayne State University Press, 1989).

25 Susan Zuccotti, *The Holocaust, The French, and the Jews* (New York: Basic Books, 1993), p.104.

26 David S. Wyman, *The Abandonment of the Jews: America and the Holocaust 1941-1945* (New York: Pantheon, 1984), pp.72-76.

27 Oral History interview with Sam Bankhalter. See tinyurl.com/kjd86ca

28 "Jumping from the Train on the Way from Belgium to Auschwitz" (Interview with Claire Probizor Schiffer) See tinyurl.com/llxd37n

29 David S. Wyman, *The Abandonment of the Jews: America and the Holocaust 1941-1945* (New York: Pantheon, 1984), p.99.

30 "Remarks by the President at the United States Holocaust Memorial Museum - April 23, 2012," Office of the Press Secretary, the White House; Corky Siemaszko, "W: Should've Bombed Auschwitz," *New York Daily News*, 12 January 2008, p.14.

31 David S. Wyman, *The Abandonment of the Jews: America and the Holocaust 1941-1945* (New York: Pantheon, 1984), pp.104-123.

32 "Focus: The Rescue of the Danish Jews - A Fiftieth Anniversary Commemoration," *Dimensions* 7:3 (1993), pp.2-24.

33 Yuri Suhl, ed., *They Fought Back: The Story of the Jewish Resistance in Nazi Europe* (New York: Schocken, 1975), pp.219-223.

34 Blanche Wiesen Cook, *Eleanor Roosevelt - Volume 2: 1933-1938* (New York: Viking, 1999), pp.284-285.

35 David S. Wyman, *Paper Walls: America and the Refugee Crisis 1938-1941* (Amherst, MA: University of Massachusetts Press, 1968), p.173.

36 Rafael Medoff, *Blowing the Whistle on Genocide: Josiah E. DuBois, Jr. and the Struggle for a U.S. Response to the Holocaust* (West Lafayette, IN: Purdue University Press, 2009).

37 Rafael Medoff, *Blowing the Whistle on Genocide: Josiah E. DuBois, Jr. and the Struggle for a U.S. Response to the Holocaust* (West Lafayette, IN: Purdue University Press, 2009).

38 David S. Wyman, *The Abandonment of the Jews: America and the Holocaust 1941-1945* (New York: Pantheon, 1984), p.337.

39 E. Thomas Wood and Stanislaw Jankowski, *Karski: How One Man Tried to Stop the Holocaust* (New York: John Wiley & Sons, 1994), p.123; Daniel Jonah Goldhagen, *Hitler's Willing Executioners: Ordinary Germans and the Holocaust* (New York: Alfred A. Knopf, 1996), pp.237-238.

40 Joseph Levy, "Jews in Hungary Fear Annihilation," *New York Times*, May 10, 1944, p.5; Joseph Levy, "Savage Blows Hit Jews in Hungary," *New York Times*, May 18, 1944, p.5; "Six Trains Carry Deported Jews from Hungary to Extermination Camp in Poland," *Jewish Telegraphic Agency Daily News Bulletin*, June 20, 1944, p.1; "100,000 Hungarian Jews Have Been Executed in Polish Death Camp, Underground Reports," *Jewish Telegraphic Agency Daily News Bulletin*, June 26, 1944, p.1.

41 Sharon R. Lowenstein, *Token Refuge: The Story of the Jewish Refugee Shelter at Oswego, 1944–1946* (Bloomington, IN: Indiana University Press, 1986), pp.47, 179; Marie Syrkin, "Free Port," *Jewish Frontier*, July 7, 1944, pp.6-8; "Admission of 1,000 Refugees to United States is Not Enough, House is Told," *Jewish Telegraphic Agency Daily News Bulletin*, June 12, 1944, p.2; "What They Are Saying: 'Token Rescue,'" *Independent Jewish Press Service*, June 23, 1944, p.1-G.

42 Henry Morgenthau III, *Mostly Morgenthaus: A Family History* (New York: Ticknor and Fields, 1991), pp.350-356, 369-373.

43 Michael S. Blayney, "Herbert Pell, War Crimes, and the Jews," *American Jewish Historical Quarterly* 65 (June 1976), pp.335-352; Rafael Medoff, *Blowing the Whistle on Genocide: Josiah E. DuBois, Jr. and the Struggle for a U.S. Response to the Holocaust* (West Lafayette, IN: Purdue University Press, 2009), pp.131-135.

INDEX

A
Aber, Evelyne   133
Aber, Max   133
Aber, Renatta   133
Actors Equity   49
Adari, Yehoshua   176
Adler, Alfred   86
Alexander, Robert   172
Amateur Athletic Union   76
America   119
American Civil Liberties Union   49
American Federation of Labor   49, 189
American Friends Service Committee   93
American Hebrew   145
American Jewish Congress   49, 148
American Legion   125
American Olympic Committee   75, 76
Anti-Nazi Bulletin   64, 103
Anti-Nazi Economic Bulletin   20
Aryanization policy   69-72
Auschwitz death camp   155-156, 159-160, 161, 167, 185-186

B
Babi Yar   144
Babi Yar massacre   143-144
Balfour Declaration   131
Baltimore Sun   8, 25, 27, 43, 59, 63, 83, 84, 86, 92, 106, 107, 130, 136, 141
Bankhalter, Sam   156
Bardeleben, Marianne   133
Barker, Lewellys   49
Bass, Yosef   145, 176
Bellamy, Francis   24
Belzec death camp   155, 161
Benes, Eduard   99, 100
Berges, Max L.   57
Bergmann, Max   47
Bergmann, Otto   133
Bergmann, Rosemarie   133
Berg, R.O.   20
Bergson Group   9, 166, 173, 195-196
Bermuda Conference   163-164, 177
Bernheim, Franz   73
Bingham IV, Hiram   127
Blatt, Thomas   155
Block, Herbert   8, 28, 31, 111, 137

Book burnings   29-34, 45-46
Bradbury, Ray   30
Brooklyn Eagle   67, 72
Brundage, Avery   75, 76
Burck, Jacob   32
Burkan, Nathan   65
Burke, Robert   46
Bush, George W.   174
Butler, Nicholas   46

C
Cahners, Norman   76
Call of the Wild   29
Cannon, Cavendish W.   171
Cargill, Jesse   138
Carmack, Paul   115, 118
Cassell, John   67
Catholic War Veterans   75
Celler, Emanuel   172
Chamberlain, Neville   99
Charlot, Jean   120
Chase, Harry Woodburn   49
Chelmno death camp   9, 155
Chicago Daily News   89, 109, 123, 124, 140, 200
Chicago Sun   191
Chicago Tribune   13, 139
Christian Century   119
Christian Science Monitor   115, 118, 119, 120
Churchill, Winston   131, 164, 166, 184
Cinderella   41
Citizen Kane   166
Cleveland Press   13
Clinton, Bill   174
Colby, Bainbridge   49
Cold Pogrom   57
Commonweal   119, 120
Conant, James   46-47
Coolidge, Grace   125

D
Dachau concentration camp   193
Daily Worker   32, 60, 168
Darlan, Francois   147-148
Darling, Jay "Ding"   8, 18, 90, 102, 108, 109, 179

Daughters of the American Revolution   125
Davar   166
Der Giftpilz (The Poisonous Mushroom)   35
Der Sturmer (The Stormtrooper)   35, 38, 39
Der Weltkampf   134
Deutsch, Madeline   185
Dollfuss, Engelbert   85, 87
Doyle, Jerry   78, 100, 134
Dr. Seuss   9, 55, 126, 151-152
Dubois, Jr., Josiah E.   173, 189
Duffy, Edmund   8, 25, 27, 43, 59, 63, 83, 86, 92, 106, 107, 130, 136, 141

E
Eck, Frank   76
Eden, Anthony   172, 184
Education for Death: The Making of a Nazi   41
Einsatzgruppen   143
Einstein, Albert   29, 45, 46, 51, 128, 130
Eisenhower, Dwight   193
Elderman, Henry   110, 122
Ellis, Fred   60, 168
Emergency Committee to Save the Jewish People of Europe. *See* Bergson Group
Emergency Rescue Committee   127
Essay on the Inequality of the Human Races   51
Evian Conference   97-98
Ezner, Maria   159

F
Fahrenheit 451   30
Fawcett, Charles   127
Federal Council of Churches   189
Feuchtwanger, Lion   56, 127
Fight Against War and Fascism   34, 77
Finkler, Esther   165
Fitzpatrick, Daniel R.   26, 62, 96, 118, 197, 198
Fonda, Henry   125
Franco, Francisco   158
Frank, Anne   125-126
Frank, Edith   126

209

Frank, Margot   126
Frank, Otto   125-126
Frankenstein's monster   182
Frankfurter, Felix   184
Freud, Anna   86
Freud, Martha   86
Freud, Sigmund   29, 85-86, 92
Fry, Varian   127-128

G

Gale, Edmund   16, 22
Geisel, Theodor Seuss. *See* Dr. Seuss
German Students Association   46
German Young People group   41
Glueck, Sheldon   195
Glickman, Marty   76
Gobineau, Arthur de   51
Godal, Eric   9-10, 38, 95, 136, 149, 158, 174, 175, 181, 182
Goebbels, Joseph   29, 34, 35-40, 46, 66, 79, 106, 178
Goering, Hermann   66, 70, 72, 79, 178, 183, 184
Goethe, Johann Wolfgang von   111
Goldbaum, Anna Marien   9
Grafton, Samuel   189
Green, Milton   76
Green Eggs and Ham   151
Grew, Joseph   196
Gropper, William   77

H

Ha'aretz   145, 176
HaBoker   176
Hanfstaengl, Ernst "Putzi"   46
Hartmann, Helga   23
Hawthorne, Nathaniel   95
Hayes, Helen   125
Heine, Heinrich   29
Henry Gibbins   190
Herzberg, Moritz   93-94
Heyman, Eva   69
High, Stanley   49
Himmler, Heinrich   154, 178, 182
Hindenburg, Paul von   18
Hirohito, Emperor   102, 181
Hitler, Adolf   8, 30, 31, 34, 127, 130, 151, 154, 161, 162, 178, 181, 183
　annexation of Austria   85-90, 113
　annexation of Czechoslovakia   99-104, 113, 114
　early attacks on Jews   13, 57, 113
　interview with *New York Times*   14
　Kristallnacht pogrom   105, 107, 113
　Lebensraum policy   139, 142
　legislation against Jews   14, 61, 64
　mock trial of   49-50
　Nazification of schools   29, 41, 43, 45-48
　Olympic Games   75-80
　propaganda   35, 40

　racial theories   51-56, 139
　rise to power   13-14, 18, 57, 113
　threat to invade Memel   103, 113
　also see: Book Burnings; Hitler Greeting
Hitler Greeting *(Hitlergruß)*   23, 25-27
Hitler Youth movement   41-42, 183-184
Hoffman, Irwin D.   44
Horthy, Miklos   186
Hosea   59
Hoss, Rudolf   156
Houghteling, Laura Delano   125
Hull, Cordell   49, 65, 96, 131, 172
Hutton, Hugh   112, 114

I

Inglourious Basterds   183
International Olympic Committee   75
Irving, Washington   107

J

Jensen, Cecil   89, 109, 123
Jewish Daily Bulletin   19, 21, 33, 36, 38, 39, 40, 44, 48, 50, 52, 53, 54, 57, 58, 59, 66, 79, 80, 87, 88, 129, 184
Jewish Socialist Bund   156
Job   132
Johnstone, Will B.   56
Jones, Indiana   127
Justus, Roy   194, 198

K

Kaplan, Martin   98
Karski, Jan   183-184
Keller, Helen   29, 30
Kelly, Walt   7
Ken   95
Kilmer, Alfred Joyce   151-152
King Features Syndicate   138
Kipling, Rudyard   95
Kless, Paul   65
Keogh, Andrew   30
Kirby, Rollin   21, 70
Knickerbocker, Diedrich   107
Knox, Frank   125
Koch, Robert   53
Koff, Syd   76
Kohner, Frederick   128
Kriegel, Annie   151
Kristallnacht pogrom   105-124, 133
Kuznetsov, Anatoly   144

L

La Guardia, Fiorello   49, 65, 125
Lambert, Margaret   75

Landa, Hans   183
Landon, Alf   125
Laval, Pierre   151
Lazarus, Emma   135
League of German Girls   42
League of National Christian Defense   81
League of Nations   73-74
League of Young Girls   42
Lederer, Ivo   190
Leviticus   101
Limbach, Russell T.   34
London, Jack   29
London Daily Telegraph   156
London Evening Standard   142, 157, 162
Long, Breckinridge   172-174
Los Angeles Times   16, 22, 61, 71, 76, 124
Louisville Courier-Journal   101, 110
Low, David   142, 157, 162
Lowenthal, Laurie   105
Lowenthal, Ludwig   105
Luke   101
Luther, Hans   49

M

MacDonald, Malcolm   131
MacGovern, Stan   180, 187, 192
MacKenzie, A.W.   188
Majdanek death camp   161
Manchester Guardian   131
Manfred, Rolf   190
Mayer, Helene   75
Mayflower   124
McCloy, John   193, 196
McCormick, Anne O'Hare   15
McDonald, James G.   73
Mein Kampf   24, 30, 33, 54, 85, 89, 110, 200
Meir, Golda   98
Mencken, H.L.   8
Mendelssohn, Felix   56
Mengele, Josef   156
Messersmith, George   97
Michelson, Frida   144
Minneapolis Star   194, 199
Moholy-Nagy, Laszlo   128
Mondale, Walter   98
Morgen Zhurnal   169
Morgenthau, Jr., Henry   173-174, 193
Mundelein, George Cardinal   125
Murphy, Robert   148
Mussolini, Benito   81, 102

N

Nansen, Fridtjof   73
Nast, Thomas   7

National Association for the Advancement of Colored People (NAACP)   75
National Farmers Union   189
National Peasants Party   81
Navon, Arie   166
Nazification of German elementary schools   41-44
Nazification of German universities   45-48
NEA Syndicate   28, 31, 111, 137
Netanyahu, Benzion   148
Neugass, Herman   76
New Masses   37
New Orleans Times-Picayune   17, 68, 91
New Republic   147
New York Daily Mirror   9-10, 135
New York Evening Post   13
New York Herald Tribune   108, 109, 179
New York Post   132, 134, 146, 161, 180, 187, 188, 189, 192
New York Times   15, 29, 57, 76, 98, 143, 156, 164, 167, 173, 185, 196
New York Tribune   18, 90, 102
New York World Telegram   21, 56, 70
Newsweek   29, 61, 98, 146
Nixon, Richard   8
Nogues, Charles   147
Nuremberg Laws   51, 61, 64
Nye, Dee   133

O

O'Day, Caroline   125
Office of War Information   177
Opinion   74
Owens, Jesse   74, 76

P

Packer, Fred   135
Page, Grover   101, 110
Pehle, John   190
Pell, Claiborne   195
Pell, Herbert C.   195
Pergament, Myles   64
Philadelphia Daily News   100
Philadelphia Evening Bulletin   13
Philadelphia Evening Ledger   107, 116
Philadelphia Inquirer   111, 112, 114
Philadelphia Record   78
PM   9, 38, 55, 126, 149, 150, 151, 152, 158, 177. 178, 181, 182
Press, Thea   105
Preuss, Lawrence   195
Pope Pius XII   154, 184
Pogo   7
Probizor, Yehezkel   159
Pronicheva, Dina   144

R

Raczkiewicz, Wladyslaw   184
Rankin, Ainsworth H. "Doc"   72
Reams, R. Borden   172
Reinhardt, Ad F.   47
Reinhardt, Max   128
Remy, Arthur   46
Richmond Times Dispatch   108
Richter, Mischa   37
Robota, Rosa   167
Robinson Crusoe   69
Robinson, J. Parker   120
Rogers, Edith Nourse   125
Roosevelt administration   10, 158
  Bermuda Conference   163-164
  confirmation of mass murder   153-154
  immigration policy   93-94, 97-98, 173-174
  North Africa policy   147-148, 150
  policy on mentioning Jews   177
  refusal to bomb Auschwitz   159-160
  response to the Holocaust   171-176
  and St. Louis   133-138
Roosevelt, Eleanor   127, 133
Roosevelt, Franklin D.   8, 9, 41, 73
  Bermuda Conference   163-164
  and British White Paper   131
  depicted in cartoons   164, 166
  and Free Ports proposal   189-192
  immigration policy of   93-94, 97-98, 113, 125-126, 127-128
  meeting with Jan Karski   184
  and Olympic Games   76
  policy on Nazi war criminals   193-196
  racial attitudes of   94, 147
  response to the Holocaust   171-174, 176
  response to Kristallnacht   113, 116-117
  North Africa policy   147-148
  and St. Louis   133-135
  relations with Nazi Germany (pre-World War II)   65-68, 128
  and Warsaw Ghetto revolt   167
Rose, Carl   19, 21, 33, 36, 38, 39, 40, 48, 50, 52, 53, 54, 58, 59, 66, 79, 80, 87, 88, 129, 150, 184
Rosenberg, Alfred   51
Rossiter, Geraldine   190
Russell, Bruce   71, 124

S

Safe Haven Museum   190
Schiffer, Claire Probizor   159-160
Schiffer, Phillip   159
Schultz, Sigrid   139
Schuschnigg, Kurt   85
Seibel, Fred O.   108
Sharp, Martha   127
Sharp, Waitstill   127
Shirer, William L.   85
Shoemaker, Vaughn   121, 124, 140, 200
Shostakovich, Dimitri   144
Sobibor death camp   155, 167
Squalus   137

St. Louis (refugee ship)   8, 9, 133-138
St. Louis Post-Dispatch   26, 62, 96, 118, 197, 198
Steinberg, Marianne   45
Stimson, Henry   189
Stoller, Sam   76
Stone, I.F.   190
Streicher, Julius   38, 39
Strube, Sidney   98
Student Advocate   47
Sudeten German Party   99
Swastika symbol   20, 21, 23-25, 61-64, 84, 116, 148
Swastika: The Nazi Terror   57
Sykes, Charles   107, 116
Szyk, Arthur   9, 132, 145, 146, 160, 161, 169, 170, 178, 179

T

Tampa Tribune   104
Tarantino, Quentin   183
Temple, Keith   17, 68, 91, 111
The Answer   161, 170, 174, 175
The Cat in the Hat   151
The Time Machine   29
The Waltons   30
The War of the Worlds   29, 166
Thetis   137
Thompson, Dorothy   57
Time   29, 98, 183
Tiso, Joseph   81
Toller, Ernst   56
Treblinka death camp   155, 161, 167
Truman, Harry   194
Tweed, "Boss"   7
Tydings, Millard   49

U

Uhl, Alexander   177
Ulmanis, Karl   81
United Nations War Crimes Commission   195
United States Holocaust Memorial Museum   174
Upham, James   24

V

Vogel, Alfons   105

W

Wagner, Robert   125
Wagner-Rogers legislation   125-126
Wallace, Henry   94
Wallenberg, Raoul   173, 186

211

War Refugee Board   173, 174, 182, 186, 189-190
Warsaw Ghetto revolt   167-170
Washington Post   8, 110, 122
Waxman, Franz   128
Weinryb, Menachem   42
Welles, Sumner   148
Welles, Orson   166
Wells, H.G.   29
Werner, Charles   191
White, George   104
White Paper (British)   131-132, 180
Wilson, Hugh   113, 117
Wise, James Waterman   57
Wolfe, Liesel   94
Wolkner, Gertrude   85
World Jewish Congress   148
Wyman, David S.   93

Y

Yad Vashem   174
Yale Daily News   30
Yertle the Turtle and Other Stories   151
Yevtushenko, Yevgeny   144
Young Women's Christian Association   119, 189

Z

Zygielbojm, Szmul   164

ABOUT THE AUTHORS

Dr. Rafael Medoff is founding director of The David S. Wyman Institute for Holocaust Studies in Washington, D.C., and author of 15 books about Jewish history and the Holocaust. He has written Holocaust-related comic strips for the *Washington Post*, the *Los Angeles Times*, *The New Republic*, and the Marvel Comics miniseries *Magneto: Testament*. He is also the writer for the Disney Educational Productions series of animated shorts, *They Spoke Out: American Voices Against the Holocaust*. Medoff won a 2014 Simon Rockower Award for Excellence in Jewish Journalism from the American Jewish Press Association.

Craig Yoe, an Eisner Award-winner, is a former Creative Director and Vice President General Manager for the Muppets. Jim Henson once said, "Craig brings with him his valuable creativity and enthusiasm. He has a nice mix of business and creative talent." Yoe has written or edited nearly 100 books in the field of comics and cartooning history. *USA Today* has called Yoe "the comic book genre's master archaeologist." Craig Yoe and Clizia Gussoni are the creators of the Unilever Corporation's internationally-acclaimed program of using superhero comic books to educate children about hygiene. More than 20 million of the comics, translated into 19 languages, have brought potentially lifesaving behavioral changes to at-risk children in 23 countries.